You're a Genius

You're a Genius

Using Reflective Practice to Master the Craft of Leadership

Steven S. Taylor

BUSINESS EXPERT PRESS

You're a Genius: Using Reflective Practice to Master the Craft of Leadership

First published in 2015 by
Business Expert Press, LLC
222 East 46th Street, New York, NY 10017
www.businessexpertpress.com

ISBN-13: 978-1-63157-294-4 (paperback)
ISBN-13: 978-1-63157-295-1 (e-book)

Business Expert Press Human Resource Management and Organizational Behavior Collection

Collection ISSN: 1946-5637 (print)
Collection ISSN: 1946-5645 (electronic)

Cover and interior design by Exeter Premedia Services Private Ltd., Chennai, India

First edition: 2015

10 9 8 7 6 5 4 3 2 1

Printed in the United States of America.

For all those from whom I have learned the heart of what I know about the craft of reflective practice:

My first teachers, Diana Smith and Bill Torbert

My PhD cohort, Jenny Rudolph and Erica Foldy

My colleagues, Peter Reason and Judi Marshall

Key scholars, Argyris and Schön, Kegan and Lahey, and Stone, Patton, and Heen
And of course, over all the years I've been teaching, my students who taught me so much even as they imagined I was teaching them.

Abstract

If you want to be good at any art form, you have to master the craft. Artists spend years mastering their craft and then their whole lives working on that craft. The same is true for professional athletes. If you want to practice the art of leadership really well, you have to master the craft of leadership. What is the craft of leadership? The simple answer is that in the same way that woodworking is the craft of working with wood in order to make things and glass blowing is the craft of working with glass to make things, leadership is the craft of working with other humans in order to do something.

While we have probably been trained in our primary craft, whether that is in medicine, the arts, engineering, or some other discipline, the craft of interacting with others, the craft of working together is usually taken for granted. It is something we know how to do simply because we are humans and human beings are social animals—we cooperate, collaborate, and compete with each other all the time. We manage to muddle through, sometimes with pretty good results, sometimes with not very good results, but we are not masters because we have not pursued mastery of the craft of interacting with others.

This is a "how-to" book for learning the techniques of reflective practice in the action science and action inquiry traditions in order to develop and practice that craft. The book explains how to use various tools, such as the Ladder of Inference, the Learning Pathways Grid, and the Change Immunity Map, for offline reflection and active experimentation in order to develop and practice the craft of leadership.

Keywords

Action inquiry, action science, Change Immunity Map, developmental theory, Ladder of Inference, leadership practice, Learning Pathways Grid, reflective practice

Contents

Acknowledgments

No work is done in isolation even if it often feels that way. Writing is difficult work that often leaves me exhausted and grumpy. I could not continue to do this without the help of many different people, but more so than any other, it would simply be impossible without the support and love of my wife, Rosemary.

CHAPTER 1

The Meta Craft of Leadership: Reflective Practice

How often have you heard the expression, "the art of leadership?" You may have noticed that it's not in the title of this book. That's not because I don't think leadership is (or at least can be) an art. It's because if you want to be good at any art form, you have to master the craft. To be a great actor, you need to master the craft of acting; to be a great dancer you have to master the craft of dancing, and so on. Artists spend years mastering their craft and then their whole lives working on that craft. The same is true for professional athletes—they spend countless hours mastering their craft, whether that is throwing a football, putting, or hitting a two-handed backhand. If you want to practice the art of leadership really well, you have to master the craft of leadership.

What is the craft of leadership? There is both a very simple and a very complex answer. The complex answer is that every theory of leadership has a slightly different definition of what leadership is and every leadership competency model has a somewhat different (although highly overlapping) set of skills that make up leadership. The simple answer is that in the same way that woodworking is the craft of working with wood in order to make things and glass blowing is the craft of working with glass to make things, leadership is the craft of working with other humans in order to do something. The medium of leadership is interactions with other people. You can interact with people to create a shared vision, to change culture, or to just get some basic tasks done; but regardless of the goal, the interaction is the basic "stuff" that you are working with—it is your material, your medium. If you don't consider yourself a leader, you still have to interact with people to get things done—that is you have to practice the craft of leadership even if you aren't doing anything that you would consider leading. Unless you are a hermit (which is hard to be in this modern world), you will interact with others. And if you are anything like the rest of us, those interactions don't always go as well as you hope. But there's also some good news. There is a secret, which you can use to get better at the craft of interacting with other humans. The secret is *you're a genius*.

Let me repeat that: You're a genius. So am I. Albert Einstein is reported to have said, "Everybody is a genius. But if you judge a fish by its ability to climb a tree, it will live its whole life believing that it is stupid."[1] And yet it often doesn't feel like we live in a world populated by geniuses. It feels more like the world captured by *The Dilbert Principle*, "everyone's an idiot" and it takes everything I've got to deal with these idiots.[2]

Einstein's aphorism is often used to suggest we should value everyone for what is unique and special about them, which we should. But we should also recognize from it that if you expect a fish to climb a tree, in addition to whatever damage you do to the fish's self-esteem, you will also be very frustrated, and when push comes to shove, the fish is unlikely to end up climbing the tree. Nonetheless, we do that every day with other people—we judge people harshly when they don't act the way we want them to, and they judge us harshly in return as we don't do what they want us to. Sure, we have lots of interactions with others that go well, but this book isn't about those—you don't need a book when it goes well. It's about those interactions where things don't go well; those times when you're trying to get someone to go climb a very important tree and the idiot fish swims around instead.

We tend to see things from our own perspective and expect others also to see the world from that same perspective and act accordingly. When that doesn't happen, when people see the world differently, have a different perspective, and act in ways that seem wrong to us, we can have

---

[1] As quoted by Kelly (2004) on page 80 of his book *The Rhythm of Life: Living Every Day with Passion and Purpose*. However, I am unable to find the original source where Einstein said this and thus I have some doubts as to whether he actually did say it.
[2] By Scott Adams (1997).

bad interactions. The good news is that we can learn to be more aware of how we ourselves and others are making sense of the world and how that connects to our own and others' actions and how to work with those differences to have better interactions. In the academic world, this is called reflective practice, and in recent times, a variety of analytic tools have been developed to make learning and practicing it easier. This book is about using those tools to learn and master the craft of reflective practice.

Learning a Craft

What's your craft? What is it that you do that is the heart of your daily practice? Are you a carpenter, a surgeon, an actor, or an accountant? Each one requires mastering a set of craft skills and takes years of dedication and hard work to master. Craft suggests the skilled practice, embodied knowing, and continual learning of what we do on a daily basis. But no man (or woman) is an island, and we all practice our craft with other people. While we have probably been trained in our primary craft, whether that is in medicine, the arts, engineering, or some other discipline, the craft of interacting with others, the craft of working together is usually taken for granted. It is something we know how to do simply because we are humans and human beings are social animals—we cooperate, collaborate, and compete with each other all the time. We might call this craft of working with others leadership,[3] we might call it followership, or we might call it interpersonal skills—because that is at the heart of all of these.

Like any craft, it takes practice and a deep commitment to master. Unlike many crafts, the tools of the trade are you. There are no hammers, no brushes, no needles and thread—there is only you, a person interacting with other people. The craft is all about how you interact with others. It is that simple. It is that complex. It is everywhere in our lives, we all have an enormous amount of experience interacting with others, and yet few of us are masters of the craft. We manage to muddle through, sometimes with pretty good results, sometimes with not very good results, but we are not masters because we have not pursued mastery of our craft.

---

[3] I have explored the idea of leadership as a craft in more detail in *Leadership Craft, Leadership Art* (Taylor 2012).

A few hundred years ago, everyone knew what it meant to pursue mastery of your craft.[4] You started as an apprentice and you became immersed in the craft, working long days in the guild workshop. You didn't start out right away blowing glass; you may have spent a year just keeping the fires going. But during that time you watched, you learned, you gradually picked up something of what it meant to be a glass blower. Eventually, you actually started blowing glass, and after several years, you graduated from being an apprentice to being a journeyman glass blower. You can practice competently on your own. You still worked on getting better at your craft, but you are not yet recognized as a master. After several more years, your work evolves into something that is more than just functional, you are recognized for your artistry, and you are now a master.

From your earliest days as an apprentice you spend time with other glass blowers talking about blowing glass. You talk about the technical details, tricks and little things that you have learned about glass blowing. When you get the chance, you study with masters, even when you yourself have become one. You are committed to the craft of glass blowing for its own sake; you are committed to quality and care for the end user of your wares. These days, very few of us do an apprenticeship, at least not in the sense of working in the studio of a master, not in the sense of beginning a lifelong commitment to one's craft. We don't speak of the craft of being a leader, the craft of being a manager, or even the craft of being a co-worker. We take it for granted that we know how to interact with others, and when situations occur that show perhaps we don't, we tend to blame the others involved. Or worse, we are the others involved and we get blamed. Or both. Perhaps we take a class and even get an advanced degree, and after a day of training, we are suddenly supposed to be good at it—if not a master, at least a journeyman.

In the arts, you hear people speak about working on their craft. Successful actors still take masters classes, and it has become cliché for an actor to talk about his or her dedication to their craft—even if it is true. It is also common to hear professional athletes talk about "working on their craft" as they spend countless hours in the off-season conditioning, running drills, working with personal skills coaches—on improving their

---

[4] For an excellent discussion on craft, see Sennett's book, *The Craftsman* (2008).

craft. That is the sort of dedication and focus it takes to become a master of your craft. All of us will interact with others in particular ways based on our experience (good and bad), family history, and natural proclivities. We will be a product of our particular circumstances, unless we choose whom we want to be as we interact with others and consciously work to master the craft of being that person.

Learning About Yourself

Let's go back to the scene of the apprentice learning his or her craft in the shop of the master. For the first few months, the apprentice cleans up, fetches wood and water, carries heavy objects—in short does all the scut work. After some lengthy period of time, the apprentice finally is allowed to work on the craft he or she is there to learn, iron working, wood working, glass blowing, whatever it might be. Some apprentices will have been watching intently, trying to discover the secrets of the craft. Others will have been somewhat disengaged, perhaps even bored as they carried water. But all of them will have learned a surprisingly large amount about the craft. This learning is largely embodied, tacit knowledge about how things are done. The apprentice may or may not know why, but he or she does know how the wood is stacked, how to keep the fire at just the right heat, and so on. Over time, the master may explain that the wood should be stacked in this way to prevent rot and that fire needs to be this hot to properly dry the wood without drying it too fast and causing cracking.

You have been an apprentice of human interaction all of your life. You have been watching the masters in your life interact. Those masters were the people that mattered to you—perhaps your parents, a dodgy uncle, your older sister, the cool kids in class. You watched and you learned how things were done. You didn't necessarily know why things were done that way, but you learned. That's what kids do—they learn, they are learning machines, and you were a learning machine when you were young. You may still be a learning machine now. I hope you are. You can be if you want to be. Human interaction is infinitely complex and interesting. There's always more to learn.

The issue for most of us is that the master we learned from—whether that was the cool kids in the seventh grade, our parents, or our dodgy uncle—probably weren't really masters of the craft of interacting with other people. To draw a parallel, if the subject was carpentry, we learned from someone who could perhaps pound a nail into a board, but probably not from someone who could properly frame a house, and certainly not from someone who could build a beautiful table and chairs. So we learned lessons of how humans interact, and they were lessons based on avoiding conflict, or dominance and power, or making others like us, or perhaps in just surviving in a difficult world. They were the lessons that make us who we are as adults, and most of us don't even consciously know what those lessons were. But we do know unconsciously, and we enact those lessons again and again. It is as if we had learned to make a wobbly, ugly little table, and now we make that table over and over—in some way we know it's not a very good table, but we also have a strong sense that we not only made the table, the table made us.

So to become a master of the craft of human interaction, we must first learn why it is that we make wonky tables. We must uncover and then unlearn our own habits. Only then can we learn new habits, new ways to interact that will be more effective, ethical, and beautiful. The journey to mastery starts by taking a journey inward and learning about yourself. Learning about yourself is at the heart of countless spiritual practices from Buddhist meditations to the Jesuit spiritual exercises. It also plays a central role in actor training—because acting is a craft where the self is your primary tool and interaction with others is the primary medium of expression.

Learning about yourself is not as easy as we might imagine. After all who has spent more time with you than you? No one, I would guess. So if it were just about time on task, you should be the leading expert in you. And frankly, you may well be the leading expert in you because no one else has been aspiring to be an expert in you. But even if you know yourself better than anyone else, you probably still aren't very good at seeing how your own actions, your habitual ways of behaving, contribute to creating problems for yourself. None of us are naturally good at this. It's really a matter of perspective. We are all naturally pretty good at critiquing others' behavior and terribly poor at critiquing our own behavior.

There are two responses to the problem of learning about yourself and both are important. The first is to take advantage of the way in which we are naturally good at critiquing others' actions. We can take advantage of this by asking others for help, by asking other people whom we know and trust to give us honest feedback about our own behavior. In return, we might offer to give them feedback about their behavior (this sort of reciprocity tends to make the process feel better, to feel more balanced and reasonable). I would suggest going so far as to form an ongoing group for the purpose. It's a lot harder to travel the path to mastery alone, not so much because misery loves company, but because others have a different perspective and can see us in a way that we cannot. Just as we would ask our partner to apply sun tan lotion to that spot on our back that we just can't seem to reach, we ask others to tell us how they see us from their perspective.

This process of getting others to give us honest feedback in a way that is helpful and useful is also not as easy we might hope. We have often told a friend about a horrible encounter with someone—a fight, an insult, an act of impropriety—and our friend commiserates with us (perhaps over an adult beverage). They go to great lengths to tell us how we were right in what we did and how the other person was a jerk. If they know the other person, they might even add some juicy details of other occasions when the other person has been a jerk—thus making it clear that it was all about the other person's jerkiness and really couldn't have been our fault at all. For most of us, this is how we want and expect our friends to behave. But such behavior doesn't help us learn about ourself. It doesn't help us learn how our own behavior contributed to the problematic interaction. Instead, it reinforces the very behavioral habits that helped cause the situation in the first place as our friend confirms how correct our actions were.

I like to call this the "crying in your beer" form of reflection. It consists of whining to your friends about what happened and having your friends support you by affirming that you were in the right and the others were in the wrong. It feels good, but it prevents us from improving our craft. It is driven by our human tendency to look for confirming data— that is, we tend to look for, pay attention to, and make sense of evidence that confirms our own understanding. In scientific terms, if we believe that all swans are white, we only look for white swans and we ignore any black swans we see. And if a black swan walks up to us and bites us on the butt, our friends will be there to tell us how it wasn't really a black swan at all, but just a rather dirty white swan and after another beer, we will all be sure that the black swan was a white swan and we will have forgotten that it needed a bath.

There is another approach to reflecting upon our own behavior and it is the second response to the difficulty of learning about your own practice. This second approach, which is broadly referred to as reflective practice,[5] is a more structured and rigorous way of looking at our own behavior. At its heart is the goal of understanding how our own behavior contributed to the problematic situation in a way that we can act upon as we go forward. This is not to say that reflective practice is about blaming ourself for all of our problems—that would be neither helpful nor intellectually honest. It is about understanding the way in which we understand the world and the ways in which we act and interact as a result of that understanding. It is about seeking a deeper and more nuanced understanding of ourselves and others in order to become better at and to master the craft of interacting with other people.

Reflective Practice in Action

Let's look at an example of reflective practice in action. Javier works in the information technology department at a medium size business. He answers the phone and it is his co-worker Scott who says he will be late because of the heavy snowfall that morning. Javier promises to pass the message on to their boss. Javier feels annoyed and quickly recalls that this must be at the least the 10th time—probably more—where Scott has come in late or left early because of some lame excuse. Javier had watched the weather report last night and gotten up early to shovel out his driveway so he could be on time. It wasn't even that Javier would get stuck with work that Scott should have been doing, it was just a more general sense of annoyance with Scott.

---

[5] The term reflective practice comes from the work of Donald Schön (1983, 1987) and my use is also based upon the action science (e.g., Argyris 1990, 1993, 1999; Argyris, Putnam, and Smith 1985; Argyris and Schön 1974, 1996) and action inquiry (e.g., Fisher and Torbert 1995; Torbert 1972, 1987, 1991; Torbert and Associates 2004) traditions.

When Scott did show up at work, Javier didn't say anything to him. They had a brief conversation about how bad the snow was and then Javier became more annoyed as he overheard Scott take a personal call and chat about his fantasy football league. That night when he got home, Javier poured himself a beer and really let Scott have it—to his wife. Javier told his wife all about how Scott was selfish and didn't really contribute to the team. Javier's wife had heard him complain about Scott before, so she was quick to chime in with examples of Scott's selfishness. By the time dinner rolled around, Javier was feeling pretty good about what a selfish jerk Scott was.

Do you think Javier was effective in his interaction with Scott? He may be a master of avoiding interaction with Scott, but the lack of interaction is problematic. The immediate issue is that Javier feels annoyed with Scott and sees him as being selfish. Surely these negative feelings will spill over and play out in the workplace in some fashion. Scott may not say anything, but I have to believe that Scott has noticed Javier's annoyance. Scott may attribute it to the snow or just write it off as Javier being Javier, but again in some fashion these negative feelings will play out in the workplace. If Javier was interested in bettering his craft there is clearly room for improvement. Javier has built a wonky table of an interaction with Scott—he could do better if he wanted to and had the right craft skills.

So let's imagine a different scene when Javier arrives home. He still pours himself a beer, but the conversation he has with his wife is very different. Instead of talking about what a jerk Scott is, they talk about how Javier has made sense of Scott's actions and some other possible ways of understanding the situation—maybe there's a good reason Scott comes in late and leaves early so often. Together they identify how Javier's actions contribute to—but are not solely responsible for, Scott contributes as well—the negative interaction. They talk about why Javier has such an aversion to conflict—where and when did he learn that conflict was so bad? The conversation moves on to how these issues may be problematic not just in his interaction with Scott, but also in other areas in his life—both at work and at home. Together, Javier and his wife come up with a plan for how Javier might behave differently when he feels his conflict avoidance kicking in. They even craft some stock responses, phrases that Javier might say when he feels the possibility of conflict and wants to run screaming away from it. And over the next week, he tries these new responses, these new ways of interacting with others, and notices how it went—what happened, how did it feel, how did others react?

This is how journeymen become masters, and how masters stay masters. They constantly pay attention to the practice of their craft and honestly and critically appraise their own efforts—often with the help of trusted others. They conduct countless small experiments as they strive to get better at what they do. They work with technical knowledge of their materials and constantly practice their technique. When they meet other masters, they talk about their craft and share new techniques. For particularly difficult issues, they may even invent new approaches—some of which will work and some of which won't. Of course, the master wood worker and the master glass blower have an advantage over the would-be master of interpersonal interactions. They learned how to pay attention to their craft, how to integrate technical knowledge into their practice, how to learn and get better at what they do, as an apprentice. Very few of us have learned the meta skill of how to get better at interacting with other humans. And that's what reflective practice is—the skill of consciously learning how to get better at how you interact with other people.

Learning the Craft of Reflective Practice

Like with any craft, you learn reflective practice by practicing. There are techniques and technical knowledge to pick up along the way and a variety of exercises that will help you do that. Just reading a book—even this one—won't do it. You have to practice, to look hard at your own interactions and experiment with other ways of behaving. Like most books on craft, this book is a "how-to" guide.

The focus on craft skills is much the same in any craft. Perhaps the best analogy comes from the world of jazz music. Jazz legend, Charlie "Bird" Parker said, "You've got to learn your instrument. Then you practice, practice, practice. And then when you finally get up there on the bandstand, forget all that and just wail."[6] To master the craft of interacting

---

[6] Many different versions of this quote exist. This version is as quoted on page 73 in *Acting Is a Job: Real-life Lessons About the Acting Business* (Pugatch 2006).

with others, you have to learn your instrument, which is yourself. You have to practice, practice, practice, which means more than just interacting with others. It means breaking down those interactions and inquiring into how you are making meaning in each interaction, and how and why you are acting and reacting. It means consciously experimenting with new ways of acting in difficult situations. And finally, after all of the reflection on action, you hope to shift to be able to reflect in action, to be able to go out there and just wail.

The bulk of this book focuses on techniques and tools for reflecting on action. It offers ways to get some analytic insight into our own meaning making processes and understand why we act the way we do. It offers ways to conduct small experiments based on those insights. As you learn and practice these techniques, it is always with the goal of transcending these techniques. It is with the goal of internalizing the methods of looking at your own behavior, much the way a musician internalizes her knowledge of scales, chord structures, and classic riffs. As with any craft, you learn and master the technique first, and only then can you forget about the technique and just wail.

CHAPTER 2

Where Leadership Happens: The Social World

Unlike most crafts that are enacted in the physical world (wood working, glass blowing, etc.), the craft of interacting with other people occurs in the social world. This makes for some important differences in how we work with our material—namely the interactions between people. In the physical world, it is usually fairly easy to agree on what the materials are—that's a piece of cherry wood, that's orange glass. In the social world, it is not so easy to agree on what happened in an interaction with another person—for example, while it may be completely obvious to you that I "attacked you," it is also completely obvious to me that I "was trying to help you." We may (or may not) be able to agree on what words each of us said, but we are unable to agree on what those words meant and what action we were taking with those words.

The difficulty lies in the fact that in the social world, it is not the thing in itself that matters, but rather the meaning of that thing, and despite how much each of us would like there to be definitive meanings for what someone says or does, there simply aren't. So the challenge at the heart of the craft of interacting with other people is finding a conscious way to work with this multiplicity of meaning in the context of our interactions. In order to do this, we will use some very simple conceptual models of how we understand what things mean. Although this sounds somewhat philosophical in the abstract, it is more straightforward in practice.

We start with the idea that our frames determine how we make meaning. By frames, I mean our theories, assumptions, and beliefs about the world. Let's look at a simple example. A group of teachers are asked to describe an ordinary classroom.[1] They say "It's a tiered lecture hall that

---

[1] This example is based on an exercise on social construction created by Ken and Mary Gergen (2004).

holds 60 students—a classic MBA case room. It has electric and Ethernet plugs for all the students and a full audiovisual setup for the teacher. It also has a video camera in the back for full classroom capture."

In contrast, a group of interior designers are asked to describe the same classroom. They say "The color scheme is various shades of brown and beige—very neutral throughout. The carpet has a slight pattern that will hide a lot of stains and spills. The lighting is indirect and artificial—there are no windows and no natural light at all. It is a classic late 90s MBA case room."

Notice that each group has paid attention to different things. And we could go on and have other groups describe the room, and they would all talk about different things (the fire marshals would talk about the alarms, the thieves would talk about access and valuables). The first lesson about how we make meaning is that our world is full of all sorts of stuff—physical stuff, people saying things, other beings—and there is always more than we can pay attention to, so we don't. We pay attention to the stuff that is important to us based on who we are. In this sense, our mental frames—our theories, assumptions, and beliefs about the world—act like picture frames or window frames that determine what we pay attention to (what is in the frame) and what we don't pay attention to (what is out of the frame). And like most frames, we see through them without actually seeing the frame itself.

With only a little bit of thought, we can become aware of many of our own frames. The teachers and designers could both easily articulate why they paid attention to what they did and why they didn't pay attention to what the other group did. But all of us have many frames of which we are not aware. Consider the Curry Triangle in Figure 2.1.[2]

It is a classic mathematical puzzle that is all about finding the incorrect assumptions that we are making. Let's look at it step-by-step. First, why is it a puzzle? This is an important first step, which is to clearly articulate what the puzzle is. Here the puzzle is something like: There are two identical triangles, which seem to have different areas. The one on the left includes all of the shapes that are in the one on the right, as well

---

[2] A famous dissection fallacy created by the neuropsychiatrist L. Vosburgh Lions (Barile, 2012).

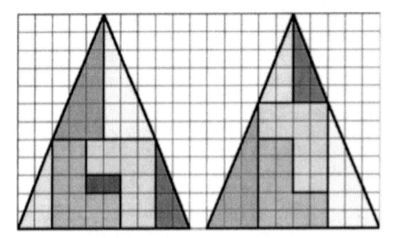

Figure 2.1 Curry Triangle

as two additional squares. That is a puzzle because I have been taught and currently believe that identical triangles have identical areas."

This first step is important, because in articulating why something is a puzzle (or problem), we have to articulate what we are seeing. And of course, when we articulate what we are seeing, we can start to see some of the frames that allow us to see things that way.

When we start to look at how I have articulated the puzzle, I see that I have assumed the shapes in the triangle on the left are the same as the shapes in the triangle on the right. In order to solve the puzzle, I need to test my assumptions and see which one is not true. I can test the assumption that the shapes are the same by counting the number of squares in each dimension. And when I do this, I see that they are the same. But of course, that assumes that a square in one part of the grid is the same area as a square in another part of the grid. I can test this by measuring the length of the sides of the square and the angles in the corners of the squares, and after a great deal of effort, I find that it's a real grid and a square in one place is identical in size to a square in another place. My assumption there is correct. And this highlights another important lesson, namely that we make an awful lot of correct assumptions. But not all of our assumptions are correct.

We could go on identifying and testing our assumptions for quite a while—there are many of them. But in the interest of time, we'll jump to the critical assumption which is that the two shapes are triangles. In order to be a triangle, the sides have to be a single line, and thus the slopes of the hypotenuses of two smaller triangles that make up the sides would have to be the same. Looking at the far left line, we can see that the slope of the hypotenuse of the lower triangle is 2 over 5 or 2/5 and the slope of the upper triangle is 3 over 7 or 3/7. We all know that 2/5 does not equal 3/7, and we now see that the two large shapes are not triangles at all, but both are five-sided polygons. In the shape on the left, the sides bow out a little, while in the shape on the right, the sides bow in a little and the difference between the area bowed out and bowed in is two squares.

So the assumption that the two shapes are triangles is wrong. It's a pretty reasonable assumption to make, since the shapes look like triangles and the puzzle is introduced as a "Curry Triangle." The puzzle works by doing everything it can to suggest to you that the two shapes are triangles. So you make that assumption instantly without even knowing you've made it. The lesson for working in the social world and interacting with other humans is that even though the majority of assumptions we make about a situation are correct, there are often a few assumptions we are making—that we are not even aware we are making—that are wrong and can cause all sorts of misunderstandings, conflicts, and also hurt feelings.

To make matters worse, we are all "behavioral hypocrites" from time to time.[3] By behavioral hypocrisy, I mean that we claim one thing and do another, often directly contradictory thing. For example, I might get angry at a subordinate for losing his cool and getting angry with a client. I claim that openly expressing anger is unacceptable, while openly expressing anger myself—thus showing myself to my subordinate as a hypocrite. This is common because we are all very good at seeing what others do, we are all very skilled at seeing things like others being angry, while we are not very good at being aware of what we ourselves are doing. This is in part because we can see others as they act in the world and we can't see ourselves as we act.

All of which suggests we need a way to see our own frames—our own assumptions, theories, and beliefs about the world—and learn how they

---

[3] The phrase "behavioral hypocrisy" comes from Quinn (2000) and is based on Argyris and Schön's (1974) conception of the difference between espoused theories and theories-in-use.

are driving our behavior. Many of the tools provide a way to do this. They are simple, analytic devices for mapping our own meaning making process. This allows us to slow down the way we think and gain some insight into how our own (and others') frames are contributing to problematic interactions. Once we have that insight, we can test our frames, much like we tested our assumptions about the Curry Triangle in the example given earlier. Our first two tools are the two-column case and the Ladder of Inference.

The Two-Column Case

The first issue is having something to work with. Memory is a tricky thing and it is extremely helpful to create a representation of particular events with which you can work. Creating an object in the world to look at, offers you some distance and the possibility of seeing yourself behave. It would be great if we all had someone taking a video of us all the time and we could just rewind and replay the video, but that's not the case for most of us. Audio recordings can be helpful as well, but most of us don't record ourselves in any form other than our own memory. So the first step is to dump that memory into a two-column case format.[4]

The two-column case is a simple format in which what was actually said is listed in the right-hand column, and the case writer includes what she was thinking and feeling which wasn't said in the left-hand column. There is usually a short introduction to the two-column case which provides just enough context for other readers to make sense of the dialogue. Of course, our memory is usually flawed, and the two-column case may not be what was actually said. But that's not a problem because our memory of an interaction usually tells us an awful lot about ourselves and that's what we are looking to explore. Here is a seemingly almost trivial example of a two-column case (Table 2.1).

I wrote this simple case and used it as an example with my MBA students a couple of weeks after it happened. It may seem like a trivial interaction, and in many ways it is. However, it is also a problematic interaction because of the emotional intensity, the anger you can see

---

[4] The two-column case comes from the *Action Science* (Argyris, Putnam, and Smith 1985) tradition.

Table 2.1 Two-column case example

Intro: I am at home on a weekday evening in January of 2004. The phone rings. I answer it.	
What I thought and felt	What was said
What?	Me: Hello.
Who? ...	Caller: Where are you and your ever-loving watching
What happened to hello? ...	the game?
So rude ... so screw you ...	Me: We're not sure.

being expressed in the left-hand column. I don't want to be angry at the caller because the caller is a person whom I interact with often and it's a relationship I care about. The caller is my mother-in-law.

There are a variety of things we can see in this example two-column case that are worth noting. The first is that we don't need a very long interaction to see what is going on. The heart of the problematic interaction often expresses itself in just a couple of lines. The second is that there is a pretty big disconnect between the left-hand column and the right-hand column. Like most people, I do not say much of what I am thinking and feeling. We don't know the tone of what I said, but even though I have studied acting, I am confident that some of what I was feeling leaked into the tone of how I said what I said. I read my answer, "We're not sure," as being somewhat cold, and overly short. I suspect my mother-in-law heard it that way as well.

Often simply seeing an interaction written down as a two-column case provides enough distance to start to see how our own behavior is contributing to the problematic nature of the situation. Often simply seeing the two-column case allows us to empathize with the other a little more than we were doing in the moment and see how their behavior was in some way reasonable. But sometimes, particularly when you are having a strong emotional reaction, seeing the two-column case isn't enough and you need to go farther. You need to analyze the interaction.

The Ladder of Inference

Human beings have evolved a remarkable ability to almost instantaneously make sense of what is going on in the situations we find ourselves in. We quickly see, hear, and smell—in short, we sense what is going on—then immediately decide what it means and we act. Unfortunately,

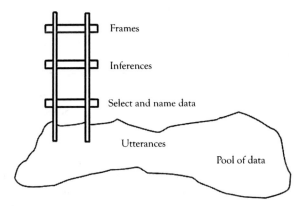

Figure 2.2 Ladder of Inference

we are not always right about what is going on or what it means. The Ladder of Inference is a tool for slowing down the process of meaning making in order to make it visible so that we can take a look at it.

There are many different variations of the Ladder of Inference.[5] We will use a very simple form of the ladder with three rungs.[6] The image (Figure 2.2) is of a ladder that sits in a giant pool of data and each rung of the ladder is a step farther away from that data. The first rung is when we select some of the data and name it to ourselves in a particular way. The second rung is when we make inferences based on the data and the third or top rung is the frames that we have that drive us to make those inferences (and thus are the farthest from the actual data). We can use the idea of the Ladder of Inference as an analytic tool to slow down the meaning making process and look at how we moved from the data to how we made meaning and acted upon that meaning.

Let's look at a simple example of the Ladder of Inference and the meaning making process in action. I am sitting in my boss's office with my boss at 9:15 a.m. on Monday morning. I have been there for 15 minutes making small talk with my boss. I am starting to get a little

[5] Including the Ladder of Inference described in *Action Science* (Argyris, Putnam, and Smith 1985), the *Fifth Discipline Field Book* (Senge et al. 1994), and the ladder of reflection (Smith 2008)—all of which may have been based in the concept of the ladder of abstraction (Hayakawa 1941).
[6] This form comes from *Overcoming Organizational Defenses* (Argyris 1990).

irritated because my co-worker Laurent isn't there and my boss seems to be waiting to really start the meeting until Laurent arrives. Just then, Laurent walks into the room. I think to myself, "The self-centered bastard is late." Now let's use the ladder of inference to slow the process down. The actual data I have is that Laurent walked into the office at 9:15 a.m. My first step up the Ladder of Inference was to select the data that Laurent walked into the office at 9:15 a.m. and name it to myself as "Laurent is arriving late." I then climbed up the next rung of the ladder and made an inference that Laurent was a self-centered bastard. I made this inference based on a frame that I have, which is that people who are late think that their time is more important than my time (thus the self-centered label) and that is a nasty and unpleasant way of being in the world (thus the bastard label). I was not consciously aware that I have gone up the ladder in this way, I am only aware that I am irritated at Laurent and I think he is a self-centered bastard. As my mind wanders, a variety of associated thoughts quickly come up. I think that Laurent probably can't be trusted to be a good team player because he is so self-centered. I think that I really don't like that shirt Laurent is wearing—only a bastard like Laurent would wear a shirt like that. And so on.

The Ladder of Inference allows us to take this process apart one step at a time. First, let's look at how I named the data. Remember Laurent walked in at 9:15 a.m. and I named that as being late. Perhaps the meeting was actually scheduled for 9:30 a.m. and I was a half hour early. My boss was making small talk and wondering why I was in his office 30 minutes before the scheduled meeting time. In this case Laurent is 15 minutes early for the meeting. The key point here is the data—that Laurent walked in at 9:15 and calling that late depends on my beliefs about the situation, such as my belief that the meeting was scheduled to start at 9:00. The inferences I make about Laurent are a little harsh and are based entirely in my frames, in particular my frame that people who are late are self-centered because they believe that their time is more important than my time and thus it is better for me to have to wait for them than for them to have to wait for me—thus a tendency to be late. I will freely admit that I have never heard someone who is habitually late say that they believe their time is more important than mine. Nor has someone who is habitually late agreed with that theory when I have offered it up. But that doesn't stop me from believing that and acting upon it. A psychologist would probably say that it is based in some form of projection and is an expression of my own inner insecurity about my self-worth and the relative value of my own time. Regardless of where it comes from, it happens subconsciously and I act as if it is true—even given evidence that it is not the case.

The Ladder of Inference is a simple analytic tool that allows me to break down my own meaning making process. When I identify how I have selected and named a particular data, I become aware that there may be other data I have not selected and that there may be other ways I could name the data that would provide a very different meaning. When I identify the inferences I have made, I become aware that they are inferences rather than facts and there is a possibility they are wrong. And when I identify my frames, I often see that they may not be generally true, and I should perhaps apply them with a little more nuance and lightness. In my example, perhaps Laurent is usually on time, and there is some reason that he is late—there was terrible traffic or perhaps a problem at home on this particular morning. Maybe Laurent isn't a self-centered bastard and that shirt really isn't so bad after all. You know, I could rock a shirt like that.

Using the Ladder of Inference

We can use the Ladder of Inference to look at our own meaning making process. As an example, let's go back to the interaction in the two-column case in Table 2.1 when my mother-in-law calls. We start with the data that I select and name, which is that the caller didn't say hello or identify herself. Then I make the inference that the caller is being rude. I make this inference based on a frame I have which says something like "proper phone manners require that when you call someone on the phone you should say hello and identify who you are. To not do so, is rude." This is a frame that I was taught back in the 1960s when I first learned how to use a telephone.

It should be fairly simple to break down your own meaning making process in this way (Table 2.2). And at first blush, it often makes it clearer just how right we are in our thinking. When I first look at the way I went up the Ladder of Inference, it feels very right to me. I feel justified that

Table 2.2 Analysis of interaction

Data selected and named	Caller didn't say hello or identify herself
Inference(s) made	Caller is being rude
Frame	People who don't say hello and identify themselves are rude

the data I have selected is named in a fair and reasonable way and that the inference is also a reasonable and logical conclusion to draw based upon that data. As with most frames, I believe it to be a basic truth and in some way an important part of who I am as a person—I am someone who knows how to behave in polite society, someone who is polite and respectful. Indeed, this identity also explains why I try so hard to suppress my obvious anger—because that isn't how you are supposed to behave in a polite society.

The next step is to consider other ways in which you might understand the situation—what other data might you have selected and how could you have named it? What other frames might you hold that you could bring to bear on the situation? What other inferences might better explain the interaction? If you're like me, the emotionality of the interaction makes it very difficult to answer these questions on your own. It is easy to find yourself blinded by your own emotional attachment to the interaction, and you see the way you have made meaning of the situation as the only possible way to make meaning. When this happens, you need help; you need to ask other people who can offer a different perspective on the interaction to help you see it differently.

I asked a group of my MBA students about this case, and they suggested an alternative way of going up the Ladder of Inference (Table 2.3). I could name the data as "the caller spoke to me as someone they knew well." From this I could make the inference that the caller considered us to be very close, based on a frame that we speak casually to those we are close to, and in fact, it would be insulting to use formalities such as saying hello and saying your name to a close friend or family member. Another suggestion was that based upon the data that the caller just started talking, I could make the inference that this was someone I know well because she assumed I would recognize her voice, and in fact, it would be insulting to me for her to identify herself because that would imply that I couldn't

Table 2.3 Alternative understandings

Data selected and named	Caller spoke to me as someone she knew well	Caller just started talking	Caller ID is commonly available
Inference(s) made	Caller considers us to be close	Caller assumes I will recognize her voice	Everyone has caller ID
Frame	It is insulting to use formalities with close friends and family	It is insulting to assume close friends and family won't recognize your voice	It is a waste of time to identify yourself since everyone has a caller ID and knows who is calling before they answer

identify her voice. Let me just add that in my wife's family, they all seem to have a gift for recognizing voices, while I am well below average in my ability to identify someone from the sound of their voice. Yet another suggestion was that my frame about the rules of polite society was out of date, and since everyone has caller ID these days, there is no need to identify yourself when you call—it's a waste of everyone's time. I didn't have caller ID on my phone, but my mother-in-law did. These suggestions may have been obvious to you, but none of them were obvious to me.

There are an almost infinite number of different ways that we could interpret the two-column case. This raises the question, how do we choose which alternative frames and inferences to work with, to explore, to inquire into, to try and hold in the future? The answer is that there are two criteria we can use to judge alternative frames and inferences. The first criterion might be called the sniff test—does it seem possible, perhaps even likely, that the frame and inference is right? In this case, it seems very likely to me that my mother-in-law considers us close and that she might think I would be insulted if she identified herself when she called. It also feels likely that she believes I will recognize her voice since she and her daughter are good at recognizing people's voices. It also seems likely that since she has caller ID, she thinks that everyone else has it (and indeed at the time of this case most people did have it). So, all three of these frames pass the sniff test. It is hard to work with frames and inferences that don't pass the sniff test—frames that our gut instinct tells us just can't be true (but more on that later).

The second criterion is based in generosity. Does the frame and inference assume that the other person is an intelligent, well-intentioned person—is the frame and inference generous in what it says about the other person? The frames about my mother-in-law that she is acting out of love, believes we are close, and doesn't want to insult me are the sort of things that a well-intentioned, reasonable human might believe. On the other hand, my original inference that she is being rude is not very generous. It assumes that she is not well-intentioned, not being polite, or somehow doesn't know the rules of polite society—none of which are true based on the many years I have known her. This also raises the question, why would I make such an ungenerous inference in the first place? Let's just hold that question as we move on to the next step, which is moving from analysis into action.

The simple analysis using the Ladder of Inference makes me aware of my own frames and offers me some possibilities of alternative frames that I might use to make sense of the situation. To bring these into action, I need a plan for acting differently the next time my mother-in-law calls and I answer the phone. The plan will consist of three steps, the trigger, the reframe, and the action. The trigger is what allows me to consciously know to enact the next two steps. In the original interaction, I didn't make a conscious choice about what frames I would use to make inferences. I simply unconsciously reacted to the call and got angry. The vast majority of our life consists of simply reacting and making meaning based on whatever frames come unbidden into our mind. The meaning making process is largely unconscious, but in order to change it, we have to make it conscious. The trigger is the method I will use that will make me consciously aware that this is a situation where I want to think and act differently than I usually do. For this example, the trigger I used was caller ID. By getting caller ID for my phone, I could now see who was calling, and I would know that it was my mother-in-law before I answered the phone.

This brings us back to the earlier question—why did I make such an ungenerous inference? Am I just a cranky old curmudgeon who likes to think the worst of everyone? Not most of the time. As I reflected on it, I realized that a critical aspect to this was that I was taken by surprise and expected to know something I didn't. That is to say, my mother-in-law was acting as if I knew it was her. When I answered the phone, I had no idea who it was, which was okay with me. When the person on the other end of the line assumed I knew who it was, I felt like I was being tested, and I was failing the test. That is a very bad feeling for me (I've had a long history of passing tests and a lot of my sense of who I am as a person is based in "being smart" and knowing what is going on), so I panicked and got angry and lashed out (in my own head) at the person who was making me feel that way. With caller ID in place, I could know what was going on, and if the caller assumed that I knew who they were, well they would be right—I could pass that test. I could once again be the smart person who knew what was what rather than the panicked little boy who was failing the test.

Once I have the trigger in place that allows me to consciously recognize the situation and act differently, I decide on a different way to frame things and corresponding set of actions. In this case, I choose to work with the frame, "my mother-in-law is family so 'family' rules of etiquette apply." The actions this frame generates are: (1) I don't expect her to identify herself and (2) I engage in a more casual conversational style in general. These frames are very easy for me to enact when I know that it is my mother-in-law calling and the panicked feeling of being a small boy failing a test isn't bursting forth into my psyche.

Stepping back a little, we can see that the big lesson here is that the problematic nature of the original two-column cases was based entirely on how I was making sense of things. In short, it was all in my head. Not all problematic interactions are all in my head. In many cases, the other person is making a significant contribution to the difficulty. But in a surprisingly large percentage of cases, simply understanding and changing how we are framing things can resolve the issue and turn a bad interaction into a good one. After doing this analysis and getting caller ID, I stopped getting angry when my mother-in-law called and didn't identify herself. The technical fix of getting caller ID provided the trigger that allowed me to reframe the interaction. It's not very often that such an easy technical solution exists. And it was a huge bonus that it also had the effect of getting rid of the source of the anxiety that was generating the strong emotional reaction for me.

The Ladder of Inference is a simple model that shows us how slowing down our meaning making process and considering alternative ways of understanding our world can resolve difficult interactions. By selecting different data, naming it in different ways, and making different inferences, we can act differently and produce different (hopefully better) results. In the example here, I managed to get help from others to get some insight into how I might understand things differently. I also was able to reflect deeply and identify what was driving my emotional response. The quality and usefulness of the analysis was largely dependent upon the group members and my own natural insightfulness. In other words, there was certain magic that happened when the group suggested my mother-in-law didn't want to insult me and was acting out of love and closeness. There was also a certain magic that happened when I realized that I felt like a little boy who was failing a test and how much that threatened my sense of who I am. In the rest of this book, my intent is to provide tools and techniques that will make these insights seem less like magic and more like good craft.

CHAPTER 3

Lack of Leadership Moments: Analyzing Interactions

The vast majority of the time when we interact with others it all goes just fine (or at least we come away with the impression that it went okay). But sometimes, it doesn't go well. We usually have a fairly simple explanation for why things didn't go well such as, "the other person is an idiot"[1] or perhaps "I'm an idiot." But as we saw in the previous chapter, even seemingly simple interactions can be very complex, and based on all sorts of assumptions about the world, it may not be as true as we believe them to be. In this chapter, I introduce a tool called the Learning Pathways Grid[2] (LPG), which is useful for analyzing those interactions that didn't go quite as well as we would have liked.

LPG is based on a very simple model of behavior that starts with our frames—the mental models, assumptions, theories, schemas, and so on, which we have in our head that determine how we make sense of the world. The frames cause us to act in certain ways, and those actions produce certain outcomes. We can use this model to look at an interaction and work our way backwards from the outcomes to the actions that produced those outcomes to the frames that led us to take those actions. LPG consists of two instances of the basic model, one in which we analyze what actually happened and one in which we analyze what we wanted to happen (Figure 3.1).

---

[1] Scott Adams (1997) book *The Dilbert Principle* is based on the idea that everyone is an idiot.

[2] The LPG was created by the consulting firm Action Design (Diana Smith, Robert Putnam, and Phil McArthur principles).

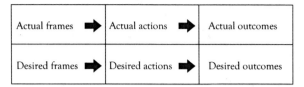

Figure 3.1 Learning Pathways Grid

In short, the LPG process can be thought of as starting with identifying the problem in terms of the gap between what we wanted to happen and what actually did happen. Then we reverse engineer what actually happened by working from the outcomes back to the actions that produced those actions and finally back to the frames that led us to act in that way. We then suggest a way to reframe the situation and enact the new framing, which is likely to produce better results.

LPG is generally used for "off-line collaborative reflection"[3] where a small inquiry group works together to use the LPG to analyze the case writer's role in a specific interaction. One member of the group may take on the role of a facilitator, in which case they are responsible for watching the time and keeping the group moving. Typically, a case can be analyzed in an hour, and the facilitator would allow about 10 minutes for each cell in the grid. The group starts with the "desired outcomes" cell and works its way counter-clockwise around the grid. This is a structured and disciplined approach, and it is the facilitator's role to maintain the discipline as much as is possible.

Because we are all experts in human interactions, we all have a tendency to jump to solutions to the problematic interaction, and it can be difficult to stay with the step-by-step process of working your way around the grid, one cell at a time. There can also be a strong tendency to focus on the other person in the interaction rather than the case writer. It is important to remember that the analysis is about the case writer, what they did, how they were framing the situation, and how they could reframe the situation and act differently to produce outcomes that are less problematic for them. Although the other person's frames and actions are

---

[3] As described in the *Handbook of Action Research* (Rudolph, Taylor, and Foldy 2001).

interesting and have certainly contributed to the problematic interaction, the point of the analysis is to identify how the case writer contributed to the interaction. The upside of this is that the case writer can change their own behavior in similar situations in the future, while they have no control over the other person's behavior.

Maintaining the discipline of working around the grid can be enhanced by using the Ladder of Inference (which is discussed in the previous chapter) in the discussion. That is, the members of the group should be clear about what data they are selecting, what inference they are making about that data, and what frames they have that lead them to make that inference. This may sound like a slow and laborious way of carrying on a conversation—and it can be—but in many cases the inferential process will be obvious to everyone. However, when it is not, the members of the group may use the concept of the Ladder of Inference to inquire into the reasoning. For example, you might say to a group mate who has made an assertion: "I'm curious what you're seeing that leads you to say that." This would be a way to ask them to point you to the data that they have selected.

"I hear a theory about the case writer's intention in that. Can you tell us what that theory is?" This would be a way of asking for someone to share their frame. Often, the person can't easily state the frame in question and it may take some back and forth to articulate it. It's also important to check with the case writer to see if others' theories about their frames feel right to them. None of us really know what is going in someone else's head—even though we often think we do.

The bottom line for using the Ladder of Inference is to recognize that we are all working from various frames, selectively paying attention to data, and making inferences that may or may not be true. We can test our inferences with the case writer and other members of the group. Doing this allows the group LPG process to do double duty as a practice field for working with the Ladder of Inference concept while interacting with others. To illustrate the process of using the LPG, I will work through an example case of Carrie's problematic interaction (Table 3.1). The interaction and analysis are taken from real life, however, the names and other details have been changed to conceal the identity of those involved.

Table 3.1 Carrie's two-column case

Introduction: Carrie is a quality control manager at a large manufacturing company. Joe is a quality manager for one of their product lines.	
What Carrie thought and felt	What was said
Uh oh, Joe can't find Rob (my boss), so he is stopping here! He makes me feel uncomfortable like he is trying to trick me … just stick to direct answers, that way he won't uncover the things I don't know. Here I go again—He makes me feel nervous so my response becomes curt, analytical, and a little "preachy." I know that! He doesn't look like he believes me; or maybe he doesn't care. He totally ignored my answer! What does he think I do all day? Most of my job is focused on reducing cost. He worked here a month before he bothered to even say hello! The way he smirks as he talks makes me feel like he is ridiculing me. I can't stand talking to him. What? This is an enterprise-wide problem, and now I need to find a solution? We are way too busy juggling with the manual system and are doing a good job. I am speechless. My escape: Don't commit until I can talk to Rob. This guy doesn't know how much he is asking … . And … I have integrated validations; I am not stupid. I have extensive experience in quality management as well and know how things should work.	Joe: I think we should validate the effectiveness of our corrective actions. They are weak or nonexistent and no one is validating that they worked. Carrie: We actually do try to validate as many corrective actions as possible. We perform an investigative review with the team and try to determine mistake-proof solutions. Joe: We must validate the corrective actions to close the loop; otherwise, we will never reduce the cost of poor quality. Carrie: It is difficult to validate because there is not an easy tool. The corrective actions are put into a text field in Eyelit, and it doesn't include a way to flag actions for follow up. The text fields are not searchable. We manage it entirely manually. Joe: Why don't you look for a way to integrate validations into your standard work? Carrie: I don't think Eyelit has that functionality now. I will talk to Rob about it.

Desired Outcomes

Start the LPG analysis in the lower right hand cell of the grid, desired outcomes. No one knows what the case writer wanted out of the interaction better than the case writer herself, so start by asking the case writer

"What did you want to come out of this conversation?" Surprisingly, the case writer may find this difficult to answer because we are seldom consciously explicit about what we want out of a specific interaction. For Carrie, the interaction with Joe was not planned, it just happened when Joe stopped by her desk. When her inquiry group members asked her what she wanted, her initial responses were:

- Support and recognition of my job and my experience from Joe
- Collaboration with Joe

These outcomes are both about the relationship between Carrie and Joe. Carrie doesn't have any specific instrumental desired outcomes; that is, she doesn't want Joe to do any particular thing, rather she would like her and Joe to work together in a different way. We can analytically divide the potential outcomes into three categories: instrumental, relational, and emotional, and the tendency for most people is to be focused on only one of the three categories. For Carrie, her focus was on the relational outcomes. If she had wanted something specific from Joe, such as an agreement to take on a particular task or provide budget for something Carrie wanted, her attention may have been focused on such instrumental outcomes. It is helpful to keep the three categories of outcomes in mind and to explicitly ask the case writer about categories of outcome that aren't present.

Carrie's inquiry group members pushed her about instrumental outcomes, but given that she would have avoided talking with Joe if she could (which we can see in her first reactions in her left-hand column), it isn't too surprising that there weren't any instrumental outcomes. However, when pushed—which included suggesting possible emotional outcomes based upon the case and then testing those inferences with Carrie—she was able to articulate that she wanted:

- To feel respected
- Not to be intimidated and have the confidence to clearly articulate her views

It is worth highlighting that the second outcome is a negative outcome; that is, it is something that Carrie wanted not to happen. It is not unusual to have negative desired outcomes (instrumental, relational, or emotional). The case writer may have trouble articulating these negative outcomes, and certainly would have had trouble articulating them in advance of the interaction. However, with full twenty-twenty hindsight, we can see that these negative desired outcomes can often be very important and show us the critical issues that make the interaction problematic.

With each cell in the LPG, it is very easy to find all sorts of things to put into the cell. It's a testament to the complexity of human interactions that so many things are going on. A critical issue for the LPG analysis process is the quality of what goes into each cell. The goal is to find not just a lot of "desired outcomes," but to find the important desired outcomes that will lead you to the insight that will allow you to act differently and get better results in future interactions. Certainly, as with any craft, quality tends to improve with practice, and over time, you will develop a level of intuition about whether you have captured the essence or not.

But before you have developed that level of intuition, the question of quality can be daunting. To assist with knowing whether you have good quality, we[4] have developed a set of questions for each square in the grid, which are intended to help you determine if you have good quality entries. The first question is whether the outcomes are directly related to the dialogue in the case. It is very easy to shift to longer-term outcomes that are not tied to the specific interaction. While these longer-term outcomes may be very important, in order for the analysis to work well, the outcomes need to be very clearly tied to the actual dialogue that is captured in the case. The second question is whether the outcomes are outcomes for the case writer. Sometimes this can simply be a matter of how an outcome is worded. For example, Carrie could have said, "I want Joe to respect me," but that would have been an outcome for Joe, not for Carrie (the case writer). By articulating the outcome as Carrie wanting to "feel respected" it puts the focus squarely on Carrie where it belongs. The third question is whether there are instrumental, relational, and emotional outcomes.

---

[4] These questions were largely developed by Jenny Rudolph and myself over many years of leading LPG analyses.

In Carrie's case, there are relational and emotional outcomes and a reasonable explanation for why there aren't any important instrumental outcomes.

Desired Outcomes Guidelines

- Ask the case writer what they wanted
- Consider instrumental, relational, and emotional outcomes
- Consider negative outcomes

Desired Outcomes Quality Questions

- Are these outcomes directly from the dialogue in the case?
- Are these outcomes for the case writer?
- Are there instrumental, relational, and emotional outcomes?

Actual Outcomes

The next cell in the grid is actual outcomes (Table 3.2). Here we ask the question, "What happened, what were the results of this interaction?" Here, it is not important to give the case writer the first shot at answering, and it can often be more interesting for the case writer to hear what the other members of the inquiry group see as the outcomes of the interaction. It is important to test these outcomes with the case writer and of course, using the Ladder of Inference as a conceptual guide for explaining your reasoning can be helpful. But do keep in mind that this process is

Table 3.2 Actual outcomes dialogue

Group member:	I think one actual outcome was that you were hurt.
Facilitator:	Okay, why do you say that?
Group member:	It's a summary of what I see in Carrie's left-hand column. You say, "What does he think I do all day?" and "We are way too busy juggling with the manual system and are doing a good job" and "I am not stupid." I read all of that to say that by the end of the conversation you are really hurt.
Facilitator:	Carrie, were you hurt?
Carrie:	No, I'd say I felt frustration more than being hurt.

meant to help the case writer, and the case writer is the final judge of what the actual outcomes were. For example, Table 3.2 shows a typical exchange about actual outcomes.

Notice that the group member saw something that they felt was important and they named it as being hurt. The case writer named it as frustration. In both cases, naming the emotion that Carrie is feeling requires making an inference based on specific data. The inquiry group member only has access to the data that Carrie has shown in the two-column case. Carrie also has access to a wealth of data—not the least of which is how she was actually feeling in the moment—because she was there. It is Carrie's obligation as the case writer to consider the interpretation of the inquiry group members, but it is also her call as to what she was actually feeling and thinking. Often an inquiry group member may suggest something that the case writer has not consciously thought about, but upon consideration it turns out to be true.

Further discussion yielded the following list of actual results:

- Frustration
- Unrealistic expectations created
- Anger
- I am evasive
- More distance from Joe
- I am defensive
- Missed opportunity to share and show him I am better than what I am doing
- I feel disrespected and underappreciated

There are a variety of things to notice about this list. The first is that there are instrumental, relational, and emotional results. The "unrealistic expectations created" is an instrumental result, the "more distance" is relational, and "frustration" and "anger" are emotional results. Also notice that there are negative results—things that didn't happen such as the "missed opportunity." It's helpful to have in mind all three types of results as well as what didn't happen that could have if things had gone better. If you are having difficulty coming up with actual results (which is seldom the case), you can go back to the desired results and see if they failed to happen.

You can assess the quality of your actual outcomes with a handful of key questions. First, do the actual outcomes capture the intensity, the emotional heat, and passion of the case writer? As a general rule of thumb, people don't consider an interaction problematic unless they had an emotional reaction of some sort and it is important to capture this in the actual results. A second question is whether the outcomes implicate the case writer, or in other words are they about the case writer (and not about the other person)? The third question is whether the outcomes are directly tied to the moment that is covered in the case. It is easy to write outcomes that are tied to a larger time frame, but in order for the analysis to be effective, you need to stay with the specifics of the interaction described in the case.

And finally, when you compare the actual outcomes to the desired outcomes, it should be obvious why this situation is problematic. For Carrie, she wanted to collaborate with Joe, and she ended up feeling more distant from him. She wanted recognition and to feel respected, and she ended up missing the opportunity to show him that she was better than what she was doing. If there isn't a big disconnect between the actual and desired results, then either you haven't captured what this case is about, or you should reconsider why you are spending your time analyzing an interaction that isn't problematic.

Actual Outcomes Guidelines

- Consider instrumental, relational, and emotional outcomes
- Consider negative outcomes

Actual Outcomes Quality Questions

- Have you captured the heat, passion, or intensity?
- Do the outcomes implicate the case writer?
- Are the outcomes about the moment from the case?
- Does the difference between the desired and actual outcomes clearly show why this interaction was problematic?

Actual Actions

Continuing around the grid, the next cell is actual actions. Here, we map what happened in the interaction. This is based on the idea that it is "what we do with words"[5] that matters rather than the meaning of the words themselves. Each time we speak we are doing something and that something is the action that we are capturing here. Naming what someone is doing when they speak is always open to a certain amount of interpretation; there is no definitive correct answer.

For the purposes of the LPG, we name the actions in a particular way. The first rule is that we are looking for expressive verbs[6] because they give us insight into the emotional core of the interaction (there's a list of common expressive verbs at the end of Chapter 6). The second rule is that the case writer gets the final say on what the verb is when the other people speak, but the inquiry group members get the final say on what the verb is when the case writer speaks. The reason for this is that the action that matters is the action that the other person feels because that is the action they are responding to. Often we intend one action and it is felt by the other as a completely different action.[7] I may intend to offer support when I tell my friend, "everybody makes mistakes," but my friend may feel it as me belittling him. Thus it is the case writer's job to articulate what they felt the action was when the other person speaks (although they may need help doing so because we are generally not used to naming others' actions) and it is the other inquiry group members' job to articulate what they feel the action is when the case writer speaks. Of course, the inquiry group members don't know what the actual impact of the case writers' actions were, but they have a more impartial view of how those actions might have been felt than the case writer does.

Let's look at Carrie's case. The case starts with Joe saying, "I think we should validate the effectiveness of our corrective actions. They are weak or nonexistent and no one is validating that they worked." Carrie hears this as an attack—Joe is saying that she isn't doing her job. Joe may not have meant that, he may feel that he is making a helpful suggestion, but what matters for our analysis is how Carrie heard it. She responds

---

[5] This approach is articulated more fully in the work of the philosopher's Austin (1962) and Searle (1969), as well as the theater director Stanislavski (1936).
[6] This idea was developed by Inga Carboni and myself (Taylor and Carboni 2008).
[7] The book *Difficult Conversations* (Stone, Patton, and Heen 2000) addresses this when they advise us to separate impact and intent.

by saying, "We actually do try to validate as many corrective actions as possible. We perform an investigative review with the team and try to determine mistake-proof solutions." For Carrie, this is a response to the content of Joe's statement. Carrie's inquiry group hears this as Carrie defending herself. The group continues naming the action for each time Carrie and Joe speak and produce the following list of actual actions:

- Joe attacks
- Carrie defends
- Joe ignores the defense and continues to attack
- Carrie concedes and deflects
- Joe ignores and dumps
- Carrie deflects

We can look at the list of actual actions and quickly see a pattern—this is a fight. Or at least it was a fight from Carrie's perspective. There wasn't a lot of yelling and screaming, but it is a classic fighting pattern of action. Attack, defend, concede—these are the actions in a fight, or perhaps a chess match (which is just a stylized version of a battle). We don't know how the interaction felt from Joe's perspective, and although it is an interesting question, it is not part of the LPG analysis. Joe may also have felt like it was a small fight or he may have simply wondered why Carrie was being so defensive when he was trying to be helpful (has that ever happened to you?). If we really wanted to know, we would need to be able to see Joe's left-hand column and do the analysis with Joe as the case writer.

We can check on the quality of the actual outcomes by answering the quality questions. First, is there a pattern of action? By a pattern, I mean that you can see how the back and forth of the actions between the two people is repeating itself or escalating or is in some other way a clear pattern. In Carrie's case, there is a pattern, it's a fight where Carrie quickly concedes. Next, are there evocative verbs and do they show the impact of each utterance (rather than the speakers intent)? Attack, defend, concede—these are pretty emotionally evocative; they are certainly not dry and emotionless. Third is there an obvious link between the actual actions and the actual outcomes. If you feel attacked, try and defend yourself, continue getting attacked, concede, and get dumped on, of course you would feel angry, frustrated, disrespected, and underappreciated. The emotional outcomes should always seem like a perfectly natural reaction to the actions.

A common mistake in naming the actual actions is to be too generic. By being too generic, I mean using emotionless, analytic descriptions of the action, such as "asked a question" rather than something that better captures the felt emotion such as "poked." The felt experience doesn't sit on the surface of the conversation; it is usually buried and requires digging in a bit. The second common mistake is to use the case writer's intent as the action when they speak. Because the case is written from the case writer's perspective, it is easy to be seduced into seeing the case writer's actions from the case writer's perspective. It is the inquiry group's job to put themselves in the place of the other person and strongly advocate for how the interaction most likely felt from that person's perspective. The actual actions are always the impact on the other and not the intended action of either party.

Actual Actions Guidelines

- Start with the verbs for each utterance
- Look for patterns, when X blanks, then blank (e.g., When X inquires, take it personally and counter attack)

Actual Actions Quality Questions

- Have you captured a pattern of action?
- Do you have evocative verbs that capture the impact?
- Is there an obvious link between the actions and the actual outcomes?

Actual Frames

Filling in the actual frames is where the analysis can get difficult for some groups. This is not because it is hard to come up with actual frames that the case writer has during the interaction, but rather because we all hold so many frames at any given time, it can be difficult to find the critical frames that are really driving the actions. It can feel like looking for a needle in a haystack. Hunting for actual frames is made both more difficult and easier by our natural tendency to believe we are mind readers based upon our many years of experience interacting with other humans. That is, most of us have a very strong tendency to believe that we know what others intended when they say something, we believe we know why they acted the way they did. I imagine right now if you ask yourself, you will have an answer to the question, "Why does Carrie behave the way she does in this case?" You probably have a theory of what her actual frames are. The flip side of this is that we are often relatively unaware of why we ourselves act the way we do—although we probably also have some theories about that as well.

Finding the critical actual frames that drive behavior, requires drawing upon our intuitive tendency to develop theories about what drives behavior as well as a willingness to explore those theories and hold them lightly as a delicate hypothesis rather than gripping them strongly as a cold hard fact. It also means staying focused on the guiding question:

> What must the case writer believe to be true in order to do what they do? What must the case writer have believed at the time in order to make their actions make perfect sense?

We are looking for frames that do more than simply justify taking the specific action, we are looking for frames that if they are true, make the actual actions look like acts of pure genius. Just as with the actual outcomes and the actual actions, it can be useful to go line by line and explore what the case writer must be thinking in order to act the way they do. This often requires some exploration of the context, because there are usually contextual factors that lead to the specific action.

Let's look at the first exchange in Carrie's case where Carrie feels attacked by Joe when he says, "I think we should validate the effectiveness of our corrective actions. They are weak or nonexistent and no one is validating that they worked." Carrie then defends herself by saying, "We actually do try to validate as many corrective actions as possible. We perform an investigative review with the team, and try to determine mistake-proof solutions." The specific form of the question becomes, "What does Carrie believe about this situation that causes her to understand Joe's statement as an attack which she needs to respond to by defending herself?"

There are, of course, many frames in play here. As a starting place, one of the group members suggested that you probably aren't on the lookout for being attacked unless you feel in some way that you are vulnerable to attack, that is, you feel you have some weakness—in short, you are somehow insecure about what you're doing. Carrie agreed that she held the frame, "I am doing a great job but there are areas where I am vulnerable." However, being vulnerable is only part of the dynamic. We can imagine situations where Carrie might feel vulnerable but not feel as if she is likely to be attacked. After a bit of discussion, the group decides that Carrie feels like Joe might attack her because she has the frame, "Joe doesn't respect my experience." There is, of course, much more to this train of logic—including the entire history of Joe and Carrie's relationship (or lack thereof), but that is the nub of the issue for Carrie.

The next set of actions is that Carrie quickly stops defending herself when she concedes and then deflects what she feels as Joe's continued attacks. Why does she give in so quickly, why doesn't she continue the battle? When the group explored this issue, they discovered that it had to do with Carrie's frames about power and authority. Even though Carrie had previously held much higher positions at a smaller company, here she felt that Joe had authority over her regarding these issues. The frame for Carrie is, "I am better than the position I am currently in, but Joe is driving the bus." And for Carrie you don't argue with the bus driver over where the bus is going.

These frames provide the big picture answer to the question of why Carrie acted the way she did, but it is often helpful to push for finer grained answers. For example, one of the group members wondered, "If Joe has the authority, why is this an attack and not just him giving an order that should just be followed?" This question led to the group uncovering the frame, "Managers should engage and collaborate with their employees" and Carrie is angry at Joe because he is not acting the way she thinks managers are supposed to act. Another group member asked the question, "It feels to me like in some way you think Joe is right about the corrective actions and part of you thinks you should have done something about it." This led to unearthing the frames, "I am afraid to fail so I hesitate to take on tasks outside of my expertise" and "If I don't come up with the ideas then I won't be seen as intelligent." The complete list of actual frames the group identified is:

- Managers should engage and collaborate with their employees.
- I am doing a great job but there are areas where I am vulnerable.
- I am better than the position I am currently in, but Joe is driving the bus.
- I am afraid to fail so I hesitate to take on tasks outside of my expertise.
- If I don't come up with the ideas then I won't be seen as intelligent.
- Joe doesn't respect my experience.

Notice that some of the frames seem contradictory. How can Carrie believe that managers should collaborate with others and also believe that she has to come up with the ideas in order to be seen as intelligent? Well, of course, we are all a mass of contradictions,[8] and it probably isn't too hard to imagine believing in both collaboration and the need for individual recognition. For our purposes, contradictory frames are useful because they can provide leverage for enacting desired frames.

Another thing to notice is that the focus has been on the actual frames that lead to the actual actions. The case writer may say that there are many things that they believe in, but unless we can see those frames in the actions, we aren't going to focus on them. This is the distinction between "espoused frames" and "frames-in-use."[9] For the LPG analysis, what really matters are the frames-in-use.

---

[8] Jack Whitehead (1989) suggests that we are all "living contradictions" and working with those contradiction is at the heart of real learning.
[9] This comes from Argyris and Schön's (1974) distinction between theories-in-use and espoused theories.

We can assess the quality of the actual frames, primarily with the question, "Do the actual frames show how the actual actions are acts of pure genius?" It's easy to go down an interesting rabbit hole and pursue our own pet theories of what frames are driving someone's behavior. Here it is critical that the frames not only explain the actual actions, but that they explain why the case writer took those actions at that time and not some other action. For Carrie, we can see how if she believes that she is vulnerable to attack, Joe has the authority to decide what to do, and also that ideas must come from her in order for her to be seen as intelligent, then deflecting Joe's attack at the end is the perfect way to protect herself, avoid contradicting the authority, and keep open the possibility that she could come up with a brilliant idea and be seen as intelligent—all at the same time. It is an act of pure genius. We can look to see if we can find contradictory frames, which we have and to look for frames that are in the form of a causal theory. A causal theory can formally be expressed as an "if, then" statement, such as Carrie's frame that "If I don't come up with the ideas then I won't be seen as intelligent." Causal theories may also be implicit such as Carrie's frame, "I am afraid to fail so I hesitate to take on tasks outside of my expertise," which could be stated more formally as "If I take on tasks outside of my experience, I am afraid I will fail." Causal theories are useful because they can be tested empirically. Carrie can conduct experiments to find out how accurate those causal theories are.

Actual Frames Guidelines

- Ask, what assumptions would you have to make, to take the actual action
- Focus on frames in-use (rather than espoused frames)
- Look for contradictory frames
- Test each frame with the case writer

Actual Frames Quality Questions

- Are there conflicting frames (there should be)?
- Do the frames show why the actions are pure genius?
- Are some of the frames causal theories?

Desired Frames

As we move to desired frames, we are turning to the question of how we might act differently in order to produce less problematic results—hopefully even produce the desired outcomes. It's usually pretty easy for a group to come up with a completely different way of approaching the problematic situation. However, the challenge is to craft a set of desired frames and corresponding desired actions—in short a different way of acting in a similar situation that might occur in the future—that the case writer will be capable of enacting in a similar situation. Because Carrie believes Joe doesn't respect her, it would not be helpful to suggest that she try and enact a desired frame such as "Joe is my biggest fan," because there is very little chance she would be able to act from that frame in a similar situation. It might well be the case that if Carrie could act from the frame that Joe is her biggest fan, she would get outcomes that are much closer to her desired outcomes, but if it's too big of a stretch, then it's not a practical suggestion. So the first rule of desired frames is that the case writer must feel that they are something they can believe and act from.

A good starting place for desired frames is to look at actual frames that might lead to acting differently if they were enacted a bit differently or were more salient in the given situation. As an example, let's look at Carrie's actual frame, "Managers should engage and collaborate with their employees." Carrie is herself a manager, so we think about what that frame means to her. In the moment of the case, it meant that she expected Joe to engage her in a more collaborative way. But Carrie can clearly see that she didn't engage Joe in a very collaborative way. So we might start by looking at how her existing frame about collaboration could be modified or made more salient so that it guided her actions in a different way. What does it look like to Carrie to engage in a collaborative way? Her initial thoughts are that it means asking a lot of questions. The group suggests that collaboration doesn't have to mean just asking questions, it could start with advocating for something. In this light, Joe's opening statement could be understood as an opportunity to collaborate with him on improving the effectiveness of their corrective actions. If Carrie had understood it as an invitation to collaborate rather than an attack, she would have responded very differently.

Carrie's frame around collaboration can be seen as a fairly positive, perhaps even generative, frame. But we can also work from less positive frames, such as "Joe doesn't respect my experience." One group member asked if Joe knew what her experience was and Carrie admitted that he probably didn't. The group member continued and asked why Carrie expected Joe to know what her experience was—Had she ever told him? Carrie hadn't and the conversation unearthed many more actual frames that were based in Carrie's many years of working in a much smaller company (which were relevant, but weren't as directly driving the actions so the group didn't include them in their analysis), but it also suggested a desired frame "if I want Joe to know about my past experience, I need to tell him." This was a somewhat larger shift of frame and, in many ways, harder for Carrie to enact because it conflicted with deep-seated feelings she had about promoting herself and values about humility and bragging. However, she could cognitively accept it as being reasonable and was willing to try and enact it. The full list of desired frames suggested by the group (and accepted by Carrie) was:

- If I want Joe to know about my past experience, I need to tell him.
- Advocacy can be the start of a collaboration.
- I can be the driver of a collaboration but do not need to come up with all the ideas myself.
- Collaborating takes many forms.
- I can be the driver of my career.

In this case, the group did not have a difficult time articulating desired frames that the case writer felt they could work with. However, sometimes it is not so easy. If the group gets stuck, it is okay to move on to desired actions. It may be easier to identify different ways of acting and then work backwards to the frames that would be needed in order to act that way. For example, the group might have suggested that Carrie respond to Joe's opening statement by inquiring about why he thought that (looking for data and frames on his Ladder of Inference) since it was different than her understanding of the situation. The group could then come back to desired frames and work on what frame Carrie would need to hold in order to ask those questions.

To assess the quality of the desired frames, the first question is whether the case writer believes that they can hold those frames and act from them when a similar situation arises in the future. The second question is whether there are desired frames that are enhancements of actual frames. The third question is whether the desired frames would clearly lead to acting differently. For Carrie, the desired frames would imply that she take very different actions, which I shall discuss in more detail in the next section.

Desired Frames Guidelines

- Look for actual frames that could be made more salient
- Look for small modifications to actual frames
- Go to desired actions (and work back from there) if there's no progress

Desired Frames Quality Questions

- Does the case writer think that they could actually hold the desired frames?
- Are there frames that are enhancements of actual frames?
- Do the frames clearly imply different actions?

Desired Actions

The final cell in the grid is desired actions, and it is the payoff for the whole analysis process. Here we identify how the case writer might have acted differently to get better results in this situation and with an eye to the future, how they might act differently to get better outcomes in similar situations in the future. There are two key steps in identifying the desired actions. The first is to identify the action, in the same way that actions were identified in the actual actions cell. The second is to craft and practice specific ways that those actions could be implemented. Simply naming the action without crafting a specific way for doing that action is seldom sufficient for enacting that action in the future—our long held frames tend to take over and we end up acting much as we did before.

We start by looking at the desired frames and what they imply for action. The inquiry group has crafted a set of desired frames for Carrie around collaboration, including, "Advocacy can be the start of collaboration," "I can be the driver of collaboration but do not need to come up with all the ideas myself," and "Collaborating takes many forms." There is also a related theme about Carrie advocating for herself in the desired frames, "If I want Joe to know about my past experience, I need to tell him" and "I can be the driver of my career," which could also come into play when Carrie tries to be more collaborative with Joe. Looking at all of the frames, the group suggests the following actions:

- Focus on integrating others' ideas together for a successful solution
- Inquire about Joe's intent and incorporate his ideas to accomplish the task
- Initiate collaboration
- Advocate and illustrate the work I am already doing

But this is only the first step. To help Carrie act differently, the group crafts an example of what Carrie might say. A good way to do this is to pick a place in the case and have each member of the group other than the case writer write down how Carrie might have responded differently if she were trying to enact the desired actions. Then, each member of the group takes turns role-playing the part of Carrie with another member playing the part of Joe. It is usually better for someone other than the case writer to play the part of the case writer in the role-play so that the case writer can watch the interaction and because the case writer can easily fall back into acting from their deeply held actual frames. Table 3.3 shows one of the role-plays the group conducted:

Table 3.3 Role-play of Desired Actions

Group member playing Joe:	I think we should validate the effectiveness of our corrective actions. They are weak or nonexistent and no one is validating that they worked.
Group member playing Carrie:	That is certainly something I could help you with. Is there a specific area that you have in mind?
Group member playing Joe:	Yes, we've been seeing some reoccurring problems in final assembly.
Group member playing Carrie:	I've done some work in my past job that might be helpful with that.
Group member playing Joe:	Great, let's schedule a meeting to get into the details.

It is the job of the group member playing the role of Joe to respond to what they feel the group member playing Carrie is doing. If it still feels defensive, he should respond accordingly—probably by pushing her harder to get her to do what he wants (a typical response to defensive feeling behavior). After the group has played out their suggestions for Carrie, it is finally time for Carrie to take a crack at acting differently. She can pick and choose from what she has seen and role-play with one of the group members taking the part of Joe (whomever she feels best captures the "Joe-ness" of Joe.)

If working from desired frames isn't working, or if the group has moved directly to desired actions because they were having trouble coming up with desired frames, you can also work backwards from the desired outcomes. The group could ask the question, what would Carrie need to do in order to feel like she was supported and respected by Joe? How could she respond to his opening statement in a way that is more likely to produce the results she wants? Again after naming the desired actions, the group would craft specific responses and role-play them in the same way.

Another method for creating desired results is to work from any of a number of different generic action strategies (which are often taught in management skills training.) For example, one generic strategy is to balance advocacy and inquiry[10] which suggests a desired action of advocating and inquiring. Another slightly more complex strategy is to balance framing, advocating, illustrating, and inquiring.[11] It can also be very effective to shift the conversation from the content to the process. Carrie might do this by telling Joe that when he says what he does to her in the way he does, she feels attacked and disrespected. In Chapter 6, I shall introduce a set of generic strategies for intervening into difficult dynamics. The critical part of applying any of these generic strategies is to apply them to the specific context of the case which happens in the crafting of the responses and the role-playing.

You can assess the quality of the desired actions, by first asking if there are specific words that the case writer would say. It is tempting to

---

[10] This comes from the Action Science tradition (Argyris, Putnam, and Smith 1985).

[11] This comes from the Action Inquiry tradition (Torbert and Associates 2004).

stop after identifying the action, but crafting actual phrases for the specific context is part of a high quality analysis. The second question is whether the desired actions clearly link to the desired frames and the third is whether the desired actions seem likely to produce some or all of the desired outcomes.

Desired Actions Guidelines

- Connect to desired frames
- Consider desired outcomes
- Consider generic practices (e.g., balance advocacy and inquiry, move from content to process, or intervene into the dynamic)
- Role play what a desired action would look like

Desired Actions Quality Questions

- Are there specific formulations of the action (actual words to be used)?
- Do the actions clearly link to the desired frames?
- Is it obvious that the action will produce some or all of the desired results?

Having worked all the way around the LPG from Desired Outcomes to Desired Actions, a picture is produced of the problematic interaction and how the case writer might act differently to make it less problematic. Generally, the first cut at using the LPG produces a rough draft or starting sketch. The picture can be refined over time with additional analysis and the results of practical experiments based on the analysis (Table 3.4).

Using the LPG

The LPG is powerful way to analyze a problematic interaction and gain insight into how your own thinking (frames) and behavior (actions) are part of the problem (outcomes) so that you can change your own behavior and get better results. Of course, doing a full, in depth LPG analysis usually takes a small inquiry group about an hour. And after an hour, you

Table 3.4 Completed LPG Analysis

Actual frames:	Actual actions:	Actual outcomes:
Managers should engage and collaborate with their employees I am doing a great job but there are areas where I am vulnerable I am better than the position I am currently in, but Joe is driving the bus I am afraid to fail so I hesitate to take on tasks outside of my expertise If I don't come up with the ideas then I won't be seen as intelligent Joe doesn't respect my experience	Joe attacks Carrie defends Joe ignores the defense and continues to attack Carrie concedes and deflects Joe ignores and dumps Carrie deflects	Frustration Unrealistic expectations created Anger I am evasive More distance from Joe I am defensive Missed opportunity to share and show him I am better than what I am doing I feel disrespected and underappreciated
Desired frames:	**Desired actions:**	**Desired outcomes:**
If I want Joe to know about my past experience, I need to tell him Advocacy can be the start of collaboration I can be the driver of collaboration but do not need to come up with all the ideas myself Collaborating takes many forms I can be the driver of my career	Focus on integrating others ideas together for a successful solution Inquire about Joe's intent and incorporate his ideas to accomplish the task Initiate collaboration Advocate and illustrate the work I am already doing	Support and recognition of my job and my experience from Joe Collaboration with Joe To feel respected Not to be intimidated and have the confidence to clearly articulate my view

will have a good first draft of your understanding of the interaction, but it will probably take a couple of iterations before you really get it completely "right." An hour is a lot of time to invest looking at an interaction that took less than a minute to happen, so of course you wouldn't want to analyze every interaction you have or even every problematic interaction.

The key to selecting cases for analysis is to find interactions that are likely to happen again, or at least the learning from the interaction will be applicable to future interactions. You are looking for cases where you have that "here we go again" feeling. If there is some way in which many different people in your life all seem to behave like jerks, it may well be that your behavior in those situations has a lot to do with it and analyzing one of the interactions might well yield learning that could be useful in the other situations.

These reoccurring kinds of interactions show us your "behavioral footprint."[12] They are our well-established ways of acting and reacting, our ways of interacting. When our behavioral footprint consistently produces undesirable results then it is well worth spending the time and effort to analyze the interaction. The LPG analysis will show us which actions and which frames we hold are behind our own contributions to these problematic interactions. Often that knowledge is enough to be able to act differently when those situations arise. However, sometimes that knowledge is not enough to act differently. Sometimes we need to know why we have those frames. In those cases, we need to dig deeper into our own personal history. Luckily there are tools and techniques for that as well (Table 3.5).

Table 3.5 Short guide for LPG analysis

Actual frames guidelines:	Actual actions guidelines:	Actual outcomes guidelines:
Ask, what assumptions would you have to make, to take the actual action? Focus on frames in use (rather than espoused frames) Look for contradictory frames Test each frame with the case writer **Actual Frames Quality Questions:** Are there conflicting frames (there should be)? Do the frames show why the actions are pure genius? Are some of the frames causal theories?	Start with the verbs for each utterance Look for patterns, when X blanks, then blank (e.g., When X inquires, take it personally and counter attack) **Actual Actions Quality Questions:** Have you captured a pattern of action? Do you have evocative verbs that capture the impact? Is there an obvious link between the actions and the actual outcomes?	Consider instrumental, relational, and emotional outcomes Consider negative outcomes **Actual Outcomes Quality Questions:** Have you captured the heat or passion or intensity? Do the outcomes implicate the case writer? Are the outcomes about the moment from the case? Does the difference between the desired and actual outcomes clearly show why this interaction was problematic?

---

[12] A term introduced to me by Diana Smith.

Desired frames guidelines:	Desired actions guidelines:	Desired outcomes guidelines:
Look for actual frames that could be made more salient Look for small modifications to actual frames Go to desired actions (and work back from there) if there's no progress Desired Frames Quality Questions: Does the case writer think that they could actually hold the desired frames? Are there frames that are enhancements of actual frames? Do the frames clearly imply different actions?	Connect to desired frames Consider desired outcomes Consider generic practices (e.g., balance advocacy and inquiry, move from content to process, or intervene into the dynamic) Role play what a desired action would look like Desired Actions Quality Questions: Are there specific formulations of the action (actual words to be used)? Do the actions clearly link to the desired frames? Is it obvious that the action will produce some or all of the desired results?	Ask the case writer what they wanted Consider instrumental, relational, and emotional outcomes Consider negative outcomes Desired Outcomes Quality Questions: Are these outcomes directly from the dialogue in the case? Are these outcomes for the case writer? Are there instrumental, relational, and emotional outcomes?

CHAPTER 4

The Genius of Self-Protection

One of the great questions of life is why change is so difficult. When we really want to quit smoking, why is it so hard to just stop? When we believe with all of our heart and soul that being nice to people is the very best possible way to act, why is it so hard to do that? Going back to the case in the previous chapter, even though Carrie believes that being defensive in her interactions with Joe is not helpful, why does she continue to behave that way? She really does believe that engaging Joe openly would be a useful and constructive way to interact, so why doesn't she do that?

There are probably many answers to these questions—ranging from physical drivers of behavior such as addiction to the insight that humans are all living contradictions,[1] or as my mentor Dal Fisher once said, "Human behavior is over determined—there are always many reasons for why someone does what they do." Keeping with the idea that we're all geniuses, the question for us is why is that behavior an act of genius? What sort of beliefs about the world must be driving my behavior in order for that to be an act of pure genius? In order to answer that question, we turn to a tool called the Change Immunity Map (CIM).[2]

The CIM is a tool for mapping out the dynamic equilibrium in our beliefs about the world that make it so difficult to change. The idea is simply that when we are committed to doing something and yet have difficulty acting from the commitment, it is because there is a competing commitment that is driving our behavior. The two commitments act together to create a dilemma for us, which we can only resolve because we are geniuses. Carrie may be committed to engaging with Joe in a

---

[1] This phrase comes from the work of Jack Whitehead (1989).
[2] The CIM was developed by Robert Kegan and Lisa Lahey (2001, 2009).

collaborative and open way, but something—some other commitment is driving her to be defensive. Of course, Carrie is probably not consciously aware of what this other, competing commitment is nor what assumptions she holds which drive it.

The CIM consists of four columns. The first column is the commitment (or improvement goal) that you are trying to achieve. The second column is a list of things that you are doing or not doing that contribute to the first column commitment not being fully realized. The third column is the competing commitment that drives the behaviors in column two. The first and third columns together create a dynamic equilibrium that makes it difficult to change. They also create the dilemma that is so difficult to resolve. The fourth column of the CIM is the big assumption upon which the competing commitment is dependent. This big assumption provides the leverage for potentially disrupting the competing commitment (Figure 4.1).

Let's look at an example, the CIM that Carrie completed to help understand the issues raised in her Learning Pathways Grid (LPG) analysis in the previous chapter. Carrie started her CIM by exploring what commitment she had that wasn't fully being realized in her interactions like the problematic one with Joe. She realized that she was committed to being a top performer and that Joe didn't seem to be treating her as one when they interacted. For most of her life, she had been a top performer, although within a smaller company, and she had gotten used to everyone knowing that was who she was. She knew that in the new, larger

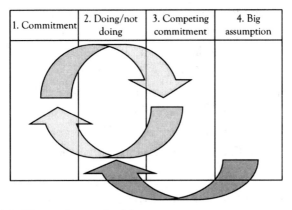

Figure 4.1 Change Immunity Map

company she was working in, everyone didn't know her as a top performer, nor should they be expected to. However, she was acting as if she expected them to when she didn't explain to others what she was doing nor did she ask for their help. Looking still deeper she could see that these problematic column two behaviors on her part were being driven by an underlying fear of being mediocre and the resulting competing commitment which was that she not be vulnerable. Carrie probably also had some values around modesty that prevented her from speaking too much about her own accomplishments, but the CIM asks us to focus on the competing commitment, which is a form of self-protection and the fears that drive it. It is the self-protective instinct and the fear that is difficult to overcome and makes change difficult.

Working from her competing commitment, Carrie is able to articulate the big assumption which underpins it; if she is not seen as a top performer and completely self-sufficient, she will lose self-respect and be seen as mediocre. It's important to note that she believes being seen as mediocre would be a disaster for her career. Her self-image is and has been for many years of herself as a top performer. Anything short of that would mean her self-image is wrong and her sense of identity would collapse. Or at least it felt that way to Carrie. And of course, when she brought these fears out into the light of day, she could see that they weren't completely true. But until she brought them out into the light of day with the CIM, they were driving her behavior in ways that she couldn't change. In short she had a dilemma. She wanted others to recognize her as being a top performer, but if she asked questions and shared what she was doing with others (which is probably part of what it means to be a top performer), they would see her as not being self-sufficient and thus not a top performer. That's a tough dilemma to resolve and your subconscious mind tends to resolve it in favor of self-protection. It is only when you can surface the dilemma that you can consciously work through it (Table 4.1).

Carrie describes the insights from the CIM as things that now seem blatantly obvious upon reflection, but were completely hidden to her before. From an outside perspective, competing commitments often seem silly, but as long as they are allowed to do their work in our unexamined subconscious they can be very problematic. Much like the LPG, there is

Table 4.1 Carrie's CIM

1. Commitment	2. Doing/not doing	3. Competing commitment	4. Big assumption
Being a top performer	Not being open and forthright with my frustration Becoming impatient and annoyed that others don't see the work I do Not communicating or explaining what I am working on Not asking for help Not responding to problems and requests until I have had a few minutes to gather my thoughts	(afraid of being mediocre) Not showing any vulnerability	If I am not seen as a top performer and completely self-sufficient, then I will lose self-respect and be seen as mediocre

a step-by-step process for completing the CIM,[3] one column at a time. And much like the LPG, it often takes several iterations to really get the map completely right.

Identifying Commitments

The first column is the foundation and starting point for the CIM. There are three different ways that we might find the commitment that we want to build upon. In all three approaches, the foundational question is, what am I committed to that I am not managing to enact in all situations? The first approach is simply to reflect on the question and think about what improvement goal would have the most impact on your life. What would really make your life better if you were able to more fully enact it? There

---

[3] This is discussed in more detail in both *How The Way We Talk Can Change The Way We Work* (Kegan and Lahey 2001) and *Immunity To Change: How To Overcome It And Unlock The Potential In Yourself And Your Organization* (Kegan and Lahey 2009).

are many classic answers to this question. For some of us, it might be, "I am committed to not avoiding conflict." For others it might fall on the opposite side of that continuum and be, "I am committed to considering others' points of view before acting." For others, it might be something as simple as, "I am committed to advocating for myself." Of course, for all of these, there are probably many situations in which you realize this commitment. Even the most conflict adverse person doesn't avoid all conflict. However, it is important that there are important places in your life where you fail to fulfill the commitment.

As with the Ladder of Inference and the LPG, it can be difficult to have the insight into yourself to know what commitment would be most helpful in your life. Asking people who know you well and a have lot of experience of your behavior can be very helpful. People who know us well—life partners, friends, family, or work colleagues—often have very little difficulty identifying things that we could be better at. Think for a moment about the people you know well—do you have any trouble coming up with things they could work on? It may not be easy to ask those close to you what the one thing is that if you were better at it would make the most difference in you being more effective at interacting with other people. You may have to do a little work to convince them that you really want to hear the answer. And the answer may not be easy to hear. But that information is out there—those close to you know many answers to the question of what your column one commitment might be.

A second way to identify a column one commitment is to work from the analysis of previous problematic interactions. As you analyze an interaction using the Ladder of Inference, the LPG, or both, the analysis will suggest different ways of acting. Your analysis might suggest that rather than advocate your position you inquire into what the other person is thinking. Your analysis might suggest that instead of agreeing with whatever the other suggests, you advocate for your own position. In the example above, Carrie's LPG analysis suggested that she should inquire and try to collaborate with Joe rather than be defensive and fight with him. Her column one commitment might have been to collaborate with others. Often the new behaviors are difficult; after all you didn't naturally do them in the problematic interaction. The CIM analysis can help identify why those behaviors are difficult for you.

The third way to identify a column one commitment is to start with your complaints (which can be listed in a column zero before column one.) If you are looking at a work situation, what are your most common (and reoccurring) complaints about work? If you are looking at your personal life, what are your most common complaints there? The intent of listing out your complaints is to see where the emotional energy in your world is and most of us have a relatively easy time identifying the negative emotional energy—in short our complaints. This method of looking at our complaints is how Carrie found her column one commitment in the above example. One of her complaints was that she was frustrated by her new boss telling her what to do when she was already doing it. She then explored this complaint to discover the commitment that was underneath it. The idea here is that the complaints are complaints because some commitment we have is being violated. The complaints act like a divining rod that takes us to commitments that are important to us and are not being fully realized. She was frustrated by her boss telling her what to do because that meant she wasn't being seen as a top performer by her boss. Of course, we have no idea whether her boss saw her as a top performer or not. It could well be that her boss had his own issues and insecurities that expressed themselves through micromanaging his people and really had nothing to do with Carrie at all. And for our purposes right now, it doesn't really matter what was going on for Carrie's boss, what matters is how Carrie understood it and what it can tell her about herself.

Regardless of which route you take to find your column one commitment, you can assess the quality of that commitment the same way. The first criterion to consider is whether it is one single commitment that is actually important to you. This is in contrast to articulating several smaller commitments. If you find yourself with several commitments, you should do some exploration to find the single commitment that is at the heart of all of the others. The second criterion is whether it is a commitment that comes from you, not a commitment that others feel you should hold or a commitment that you think you should have, but deep down inside you really don't feel very attached to it. The third criterion is that the commitment shouldn't be fully realized in your life. That is, there should be places in your life where you don't manage to fully enact the commitment. The fourth criterion is that the commitment should be specific enough so that you can tell whether you are enacting it or not. You may be committed to being a nice person, but it is awfully difficult to tell if you are managing to be nice in your interactions with others. It is much easier to work with a more specific concept such as advocating for yourself or not avoiding conflict. The final criterion is that the commitment should implicate you in the action. You might well be committed to other people being nicer to you, but that is a commitment that isn't something you can enact, it depends on other people enacting it.

Column One Commitment Guidelines

- What would you like to get better at or improve on?
- What commitment would help you enact your plan of inquiry?
- What commitment lies underneath your common complaints?

Column One Commitment Quality Criteria

- One big thing that is important to you
- Should be a commitment you actually hold (not one you feel you should hold)
- Should be a commitment that is not currently fully realized
- Be specific enough
- Should implicate yourself in the commitment (not be about other people changing)

What You're Doing/Not Doing

The second column in the CIM is titled "doing/not doing" and is a list of things that you are doing and things you are not doing that are preventing your column one commitment from being fully realized. It is not two different lists (one of things you are doing and the other of things you are not doing), but is titled "doing/not doing" in the recognition that sins of omission can be just as important as sins of commission. In short, the column is filled with a list of behavior, of things that you do or fail to do that run counter to your column one commitment.

A good place to start is to recognize that you probably do a lot of things to realize your column one commitment. If you are committed to advocating for yourself, there are probably many places where you successfully do just that. Congratulations to you, you should feel good about all of the things you do to realize your column one commitment. Go ahead and pat yourself on the back and bask in the warmth of being proud of yourself for doing a good job. It's important to recognize that you do a lot to realize your column one commitment for two reasons. The first is that it is easier to admit to yourself all of the negative ways in which you do or don't do things that prevent you from fully realizing your column one commitment when you recognize that you are doing a lot of positive things to enact your commitment. The second reason is that recognizing the many ways in which you enact your commitment allows you to start to inquire into the contextual factors that may be affecting your commitment. Why do I have no problem avoiding conflict with my family, but a huge problem with avoiding conflict at work? What is the difference between the two environments that makes a difference for me?

Filling out this column can be difficult. Humans are very good at seeing how other people's actions lead to particular results; we are often blind to how our own actions lead to results we don't want. The key here is to focus on specific actions that are contrary to the column one commitment. If I am committed to not avoiding conflict, then when I agree with someone who I don't really agree with in order to avoid conflict I should list that as something I am doing in column two. If I am committed to understanding others' perspectives and I don't really listen to what they are saying, I should list that in column two. Those actions may seem incredibly obvious, but generating a good list lays the foundation for the next column, which is where the useful insights start to happen.

You can tell if you have high quality entries in the "doing/not doing" column by looking at the quality criteria. The first criterion is whether the behavior listed is concrete and particular. The more specific the behavior, the more useful it will be later. For example, "I don't listen to what others say" is better than "Not paying attention." The second criterion is that each entry is a behavior, something that a third party who is present could observe. There is a temptation to simply report an inner feeling state. Instead of saying "be afraid," you would want to list what you do when you feel afraid, such as "agree with whatever my boss says even though

I don't actually agree with him." The third criterion is that you should be able to easily explain how the behaviors in column two run counter to or conflict with your column one commitment.

Doing/Not Doing Guidelines

- What are you doing/not doing that prevents your commitment from being fully realized
- Recognize that you are doing a lot to realize it, look at what you are doing that gets in the way
- This is hard for most people, we're often blind to how our own actions produce results we don't want (but good at seeing others)

Doing/Not Doing Quality Criteria

- Concreteness and particularity
- Examples of real specific behaviors (not just feelings)
- Be able to explain how behaviors run counter to or conflict with column one commitment

Competing Commitments

The third column of the CIM is the competing commitment. The competing commitment is what drives your column two behaviors. It is what prevents you from fully enacting your column one commitment. And by and large most of us aren't consciously aware that we hold the competing commitment. Competing commitments are a commitment to protect yourself in some way. They are based in a fear that something horrible will happen if you stop doing your column two behaviors. The way to discover the competing commitment is start by looking for the fear. How would it feel if you didn't do the column two behaviors or did do the things you aren't doing? What are you afraid would happen if you don't do the things you are doing in column two or did do the things you aren't doing? Once you've identified the fear, your competing commitment is to prevent whatever you are afraid of from happening.

As an example, let me tell you a brief story of finding one of my own competing commitments. I was coteaching an action research class in Denmark and when we asked the students for some feedback on how the class was going, they said that they wished we could go into more depth with the different topics. It felt like just when we really started to get into something it was time to move on to the next topic. I realized that I shared their complaint about not going into the topics in as much depth as I would have liked to. As one of the instructors and designers of the class, I had a lot of say about what we covered and how long we spent on each topic so it was pretty clear to me that I had a lot of culpability. I decided to explore the issue with the CIM.

Starting with the complaint, I thought about what commitment I held that was being violated. It was relatively easy for me to identify that I was committed to covering topics in real depth, particularly when working with doctoral students, as I was in this case. Moving on to column two, again it was fairly easy to see that I was not allowing enough time to explore some of the subjects in sufficient depth and scheduling too many different topics to allow indepth exploration of all (or even many, or maybe even any) of them. No real surprises so far. Now for the competing commitment—What was I afraid of? I thought about it and quickly realized that I was afraid that we wouldn't cover important materials, I was afraid that if I didn't keep moving along we wouldn't get to all of the topics that I felt were important to cover. And it would have been easy to stop there. It was a simple and classic dilemma between breadth and depth. I was committed to covering the subjects in depth and also covering a breadth of topics and clearly there had to be a trade-off between the two given the time constraints of the class. Perhaps I had made the wrong trade-off and would want to change the balance a bit in the future, but the trade-off itself was unavoidable. I started to feel a little better about myself.

But I also knew that the competing commitment to cover all of the material felt almost noble (it was fighting the good fight in some way) and it wasn't really a form of self-protection—two important criteria for a good competing commitment. I needed to look deeper, I needed to find the fear that was about me, what was I afraid would happen to me—not what would happen to the students, not what would happen to my task of teaching an action research class, but what would happen to me personally. What would happen to me if I didn't push on to the next topic and allowed time to really go into a topic in depth? What was I afraid would happen?

It's important to know that fears don't tend to be rational. They don't make sense, so we can't find them through analysis. We find the fear by paying attention to how we feel. We find the fear by allowing our imagination to pretend to be in that situation and see what happens. Let the situation play out and see what happens that makes your stomach go queasy with fear. It is different for each one of us. George Orwell, in his classic book *1984*, puts that fear in Room 101.

"You asked me once," said O'Brien, "what was in Room 101. I told you that you knew the answer already. Everyone knows it. The thing that is in Room 101 is the worst thing in the world."

The door opened again. A guard came in, carrying something made of wire, a box or basket of some kind. He set it down on the further table. Because of the position in which O'Brien was standing, Winston could not see what the thing was.

"The worst thing in the world," said O'Brien, "varies from individual to individual. It may be burial alive, or death by fire, or by drowning, or by impalement, or fifty other deaths. There are cases where it is some quite trivial thing, not even fatal."

He had moved a little to one side, so that Winston had a better view of the thing on the table. It was an oblong wire cage with a handle on top for carrying it by. Fixed to the front of it was something that looked like a fencing mask, with the concave side outwards. Although it was three or four metres away from him, he could see that the cage was divided lengthways into two compartments, and that there was some kind of creature in each. They were rats.

"In your case," said O'Brien, "the worst thing in the world happens to be rats."

A sort of premonitory tremor, a fear of he was not certain what, had passed through Winston as soon as he caught his first glimpse of the cage. But at this moment the meaning of the mask-like attachment in front of it suddenly sank into him. His bowels seemed to turn to water.

"You can't do that!" he cried out in a high cracked voice. "You couldn't, you couldn't! It's impossible."

"Do you remember," said O'Brien, "the moment of panic that used to occur in your dreams? There was a wall of blackness in front of you, and a roaring sound in your ears. There was something terrible on the other side of the wall. You knew that you knew what it was, but you dared not drag it into the open. It was the rats that were on the other side of the wall."[4]

Not every competing commitment is based in a fear as deep as Winston's fear of rats, but that does capture the essence of the sort of irrational, existential fear that you are looking for. It needs to be a fear of something horrible that will happen to you, to your very self. Some common fears are the fear of being a failure, of being alone, of not being liked by others—it all depends on what matters to you and to your sense of self.

So what existential fear was at play for me? What did I fear would happen if we went deep into one subject and didn't move on to the next topic? I was afraid that the students would find out that I was a fraud. It's that simple and for me that terrifying. I can feel my pulse race as I type and it's all I can do to keep writing these words. But you have to face your fear to overcome it and sharing this experience is part of how I work to overcome that fear. I was afraid that the students would find out that my knowledge and experience had limits; that is, if pushed deeply enough, I wouldn't know all the answers. This was horrible because of my long held sense of identity as the smart guy. Growing up, I had always been the smart kid. I had been praised and rewarded for being the smart kid. But none of us are smart enough to know everything, and I also knew that my knowledge had limits. The thought of having those limits exposed was horrifying.

Notice that the fear has an all or nothing sort of identity construction. Either I am the smart guy or I am not. If there is some way in which I am not the smart guy, then I am not the smart guy in everything—there is not the possibility of being somewhat smart or pretty smart. I know intellectually that this all or nothing identity construction is ridiculous, but nonetheless it is how my subconscious constructs it. And it is not unusual

---

[4] From Part 3, Chapter 5 (Orwell 1949).

for your subconscious to construct important aspects of your identity this way. Either you are a good person or not. Either you are a smart person or not. None of these all or nothing constructions will stand up to the light of day, but as long as they stay in the darkness of your subconscious they can drive our fears and our actions.

I'm also aware that I am ashamed that I am afraid to be found out to be a fraud. I have consciously chosen to approach teaching as "the guide on the side" rather than "the sage on the stage." I believe in saying, "I don't know, let's figure it out," when a student asks me a question and I don't know the answer. And that has happened many times. I am ashamed that my behavior is being driven by this fear that I thought I had conquered. This too is typical of strong competing commitments. They feel familiar and often a little creepy. The fear of being a fraud echoes the panicked little boy who felt like he was failing the test in chapter two. I suspect I will never completely get over that fear. A large part of my identity will always be about being the smart guy and whenever that identity is threatened I will act to defend it. I will find clever ways to protect that identity such as stuffing 10 pounds of content into a five pound bag of a class and telling myself that it's the classic trade-off between depth and breadth—which when you look at it really is an act of genius.

It can be difficult to work directly with the fear and the commitment to prevent that fear from happening. I don't like admitting that I am afraid of being found out to be a fraud and the negative commitment doesn't suggest many other possibilities. It may be easier to recraft the commitment into a positive form. Rather than saying what you don't want to happen, what do you want to happen? The flip side of not wanting to be found out to be fraud is that I am committed to being seen as a smart and competent expert in my field. That commitment suggests a variety of possibilities and is certainly a lot easier to say to myself and others. It does have a somewhat noble ring to it and doesn't feel problematic in itself. In order to understand the problematic nature I need to keep the fear and the self-protective nature of it in mind.

Some common fears are:

- Looking stupid
- Being rejected

- Letting others down;
- Looking weak and ineffective;
- Looking selfish;
- Being seen as controlling or a micromanager;
- Failing, being a loser;
- Looking bad;
- Feeling vulnerable;
- Being alone;
- Showing what I care about, what I can do;
- Not being liked by people;
- Looking like I think I am superior; and
- Something going wrong and it will be my fault.

Competing Commitment Guidelines

- Start with your fear of what will happen if you don't do the previous column
- How would opposite of column two doing/not doing behavior feel?
- Active commitment to keep that fear from happening should be some form of self-protection

Competing Commitment Quality Criteria

- Should be a form of self-protection
- Competes with column one
- Fear links to column two and shows why column two behaviors are brilliant!
- One good counter commitment (as opposed to many mediocre ones)
- Doesn't have a "noble" ring to it
- Should creep you out a little (recognize it from the past)

Big Assumptions

The fourth column is the big assumption that is the foundation of the competing commitment. It is called the big assumption because we tend

to act as if it is true. We are also usually unconscious that we hold the assumption—it is a simple, taken-for-granted fact of our existence such as the sun rising in the east. The big assumption is stated in the form of an "if, then" statement. This form allows you to test and explore the big assumption. For example, Carrie's big assumption in the first example is "If I am not seen as a top performer and completely self-sufficient, then I will lose self-respect and be seen as mediocre." This may sound ridiculous to you and me, but for Carrie it was a simple fact of her existence. We should recognize that your big assumption may have a grain of truth in it, after all it did come from somewhere, from some experience you have had in the world. But your subconscious has taken the grain of truth and expanded it into something much bigger—a theory that applies everywhere and is treated as a fact.

The big assumption consists of two parts, the "if" part and the "then" part. The "then" part is something truly horrible. For Carrie, losing self-respect and being seen as mediocre is horrible. It is what is in room 101 for her. It doesn't matter that the laws of statistics tell us that most of us are mediocre—in the sense of being average or near average in most ways—and manage to get along just fine. There are probably many ways in which Carrie is mediocre. But her sense of who she is, her sense of identity is all about being a top performer and anything less would be crushing—she would no longer be who she believes herself to be. So, for Carrie the "then" of being seen as mediocre is a truly horrible and real existential threat to her identity.

We can articulate the big assumption in a couple of different ways. One way is to start with the competing commitment and say, if I do not "competing commitment," then something really bad will happen. Continuing with my own example, this would be "if I am not seen as an intelligent and competent professional, then I am a failure." The idea of being a failure is horrible to me. Again, in writing these words I feel my heart race and a bead of sweat forms on the back of my neck. Which isn't to say I have never failed. I have failed many times, and I have learned a lot from those failures. Nonetheless, the idea of being seen as a failure horrifies me. I wonder if I could bare it.

The second way to articulate the big assumption is to say, if I don't engage in the column two behaviors, then my column three fear will

happen. In my example, this would be, "If I allowed sufficient time to cover the topics in-depth, then I would be found out to be a fraud." Either way of articulating the big assumption generates a testable, causal theory. The first method gave us a slightly more general big assumption, while the second method offered a big assumption that was more tightly tied to the original scenario. Both give us plenty of insight into what was driving my behavior and how my actions showed I was a genius—a genius at protecting myself, as most of us tend to be. The completed CIM is shown in Table 4.2.

We can judge the quality of the big assumption on a few criteria. The first criterion is that it is a causal relationship, which is specified by the "if, then" structure. The second criterion is that the second half of the "if, then" statement is something that is really bad. It doesn't have to be something that is generically bad, but it does have to be something that feels absolutely horrible for the person who is analyzing their self. The third criteria is that it is testable, which simply means that there is some way in which we could test the assumption. There must be the possibility of finding disconfirming data. The fourth criterion is that it shows us a valuable way to disturb the dynamic stability that has been created by the tension between the column one commitment

Table 4.2 Steve's CIM

0. Complaints	1. Commitment	2. Doing/ not doing	3. Competing commitment	4. Big assumption
Not going into topics in sufficient depth Running out of time to explore topics	Committed to covering topics in real depth	Not allowing enough time to explore some of the subjects in sufficient depth scheduling too many different topics to allow in-depth exploration of all	(Afraid of being found out to be a fraud) To be seen as an intelligent and competent professional	If I am not seen as an intelligent and competent professional, then I am a failure; if I allowed sufficient time to cover the topics in-depth, then I would be found out to be a fraud

and the competing commitment. Let's look at these last two in relation to my CIM.

If I can find some disconfirming data, it allows me to question the truth of the big assumption. It also allows me to start to tame my big assumption. By taming the big assumption, I mean to change it from a wild beast that applies everywhere to a more controlled domestic animal that knows where it belongs and where it doesn't. It would be nice to be able to get rid of it completely, but that is very difficult, so we start with the ambition of simply taming it.

The first step is to look for disconfirming data. This can start simply by thinking about cases from the past where the first half of the big assumption happened. If I think back, are there times where I was not seen as a professional and competent professional? Are there times where I went into sufficient depth with a subject? And of course, the answer is yes to both questions. So what happened in those cases? Was I failure? Was I found out to be a fraud? And of course there are two ways that can go, either yes I was a failure or discovered to be a fraud or no I wasn't. If my big assumption was correct and I was a failure, then I have some data on what it is like to be a failure, and perhaps, some evidence that being a failure isn't quite so horrible as I think and that at the very least I seem to have survived it—emotionally scarred, but still here. If my big assumption wasn't correct and I wasn't a failure or found out to be a fraud, then I have some evidence that my big assumption isn't always correct and I can ask the next question—When and where does my big assumption apply?

When I explored these questions farther, I realized that there were particular contextual factors that had evoked my big assumption. In most of my teaching I didn't have a fear of being discovered to be a fraud. However, I do have some real insecurity about my knowledge of philosophy and many of the students had their undergraduate degrees in philosophy. I was afraid that if the discussion went deep they would discover that they knew much more than I do about philosophy. And when I realized that, something interesting happened—I was no longer afraid. I am okay with people who have studied philosophy knowing more about it than I do. I may have a PhD, but I am not a philosopher and I am okay with that. My big assumption has been tamed, I know what is at the heart of it and

where it applies and where it doesn't. I can use that knowledge to disturb my own immunity to change.

Big Assumption Guidelines

- I assume that if I do not do "competing commitment" then blank will happen (blank is something really bad)
- (Alternatively) if I don't engage in column two behaviors, the column three fear will happen

Big Assumption Quality Criteria

- Specific causal relationship
- Second part of causal relationship is big time bad
- Is testable in some way (that is disconfirmable)
- Shows us some valuable way to disturb the system

Looking for the Genius in Yourself and Others

The CIM is a tool for uncovering and working with the complexity of the various commitments and motivations that drive us. It highlights the ways in which our drive for self-preservation can play a central role in our inability to do what we think we really want to do. It is an excellent tool for understanding our own behavior and overcoming our own immunity to change. But it is also more than that, it is an illustration of the foundational idea of this book—namely that you're a genius.

The CIM shows us a particular type of genius. It shows us ways in which our own actions are acts of the genius of self-protection. It also illustrates in a broader sense how even actions that seem to be fundamentally stupid from one perspective are actually brilliant from another perspective. If we are to understand our own behavior, we must understand how our own actions our acts of genius. To understand others' behavior, we should try and understand how their actions are acts of genius.

It is not easy to approach the world with the belief that everyone is a genius. It is the ultimate generous inference. If you can manage to do it, it leads to empathy for and connection with others rather than anger

and disgust. This is a critical point in enacting the idea that everyone is a genius in your life. It is easy to use the logic of the CIM to gain a great deal of insight into yourself and others. And it can be easy to follow that insight with harsh judgment for both yourself and others. I can easily find myself saying, "What an idiot you are, Steve for being afraid of being found out to be a fraud by a bunch of Danish graduate students." But that's not very generous (and yes it is just as important to be generous and empathetic for yourself as it to be generous and empathetic to others.) I can also find myself feeling sorry for myself, saying, "Oh, Steve, that really sucks that somewhere at you innermost core you are such a miserable and insecure creature." That's not very generous either. Both the "poor, baby" and "you're an idiot" are based in a standard that suggests we shouldn't be the way we are, we should be better. If you spend your life expecting yourself and others to be better than what we are, you will often be disappointed. That isn't to say that you shouldn't try to be better than you are, simply that you shouldn't punish yourself and others for not being better than what we are.

The same can be said for how we approach others. Of course, we usually can only guess at what fears and competing commitments drive others' actions, and the point here is not that we should try and figure out what others' competing commitments are, but rather that we should assume that they are rational people, acting from reasons that we (and perhaps they) don't understand. This belief is the foundation of a shift from judging others to being curious about them (more about that shift in Chapter 7). The shift is fundamental for improving our own craft of interacting with others. It is perhaps the most difficult challenge in the world to be really curious about those other people who really make us angry. For me, it is the essence of acting lovingly to those whom it is hardest to act lovingly toward (Table 4.3).

Table 4.3 Short guide for CIM analysis

1. Commitment	2. Doing/not doing	3. Competing commitment	4. Big assumption
Guidelines	*Guidelines*	*Guidelines*	*Guidelines*
What would you like to get better at and improve on? What commitment would help you enact your plan of inquiry? What commitment lies underneath your common complaints? *Quality criteria* One big thing that is important to you Should be a commitment you actually hold (not one you feel you should hold) Should be a commitment that is not currently fully realized Be specific enough Should implicate yourself in the commitment (not be about other people changing)	What are you doing and not doing that prevents your commitment from being fully realized Recognize that you are doing a lot to realize it, look at what you are doing that gets in the way This is hard for most people, we're often blind to how our own actions produce results we don't want (but good at seeing others) *Quality criteria* Concreteness and Particularity Examples of real specific behaviors (not just feelings) Be able to explain how behaviors runs counter to or conflicts with column one commitment	Start with your fear of what will happen if you don't do the previous column How would opposite of column two doing/not doing behavior feel? Active commitment to keep that fear from happening should be some form of self-protection *Quality criteria* Should be a form of self-protection Competes with column one Fear links to column two and shows why column two behaviors are brilliant! One good counter commitment (as opposed to many mediocre ones) Doesn't have a "noble" ring to it Should creep you out a little (recognize it from the past)	I assume that if I do not "competing commitment" then blank will happen" (blank is usually something really bad) (Alternatively) if I don't engage in column two behaviors, the column three fear will happen *Quality criteria* Specific causal relationship Second part of causal relationship is big time bad Is testable in some way (that is disconfirmable) Shows us some valuable way to disturb the system

CHAPTER 5

Working on Your Own Leadership: Practice Experiments

For most of us the word experiment conjures up an image of a scientist in a laboratory. The scientist carefully follows a procedure, perhaps mixing together a batch of chemicals and then tests the resulting liquid to see how well it works as a glue. The scientist then repeats the same process making one change, perhaps a different chemical or a different amount of one of the chemicals, and repeats the tests to see if the second liquid works better or worse as a glue.

These sorts of experiments are done in the techno-rational[1] tradition and are based on a variety of assumptions about the world. They assume that things behave the same way under the same conditions—if I drop a ball and it falls to earth at a certain speed, the next time I drop the ball it will also fall to earth at that speed. They also assume that it is possible to act from outside the system that is being studied in a way that doesn't affect the system being studied. The experiments are designed to test a hypothesis or theory that the scientist has with the general goal of gaining knowledge that can be used to control and optimize the system in the future. When the scientist learns which combination of chemicals makes the best glue, he can then go off and make the best glue time after time.

This sort of experimenting is invaluable for learning about the physical world where the assumptions hold true. However, in the social world it is almost impossible to change just one variable while holding all of

---

[1] This categorization of experiments comes in large part from *The Reflective Practitioner* (Schön 1983).

the others constant.[2] In the social world, people don't always do the same thing in the same situation. And it is impossible to act from outside the system—you are always part of the system. Thus in the realm of human interaction, you need a different type of experiment, a practice experiment. Practice experiments can also be about testing a hypothesis, but they are based on the assumptions that you are always part of the system and it's a complex system that is not governed by simple relationships that are easily defined. In practice experiments, you try acting differently and see what happens. Your goal is not to gain knowledge with the intent of optimization and control in the future. With a practice experiment, your goal is to gain greater understanding of the specific situation and hopefully to transform the situation from one that is problematic in some way to one that is not problematic or at least significantly less so.

We can think of acting in the social world as an ongoing experiment. Every action is also an inquiry and every inquiry is also an action.[3] For example, when I walk into the office first thing in the morning and I say, "good morning" to Larson, the administrative assistant, it is also a test of the microsocial world of the office. Is it the usual, status quo where Larson responds with "good morning" and nothing more? Or is there something different today? Perhaps Larson responds by saying, "I don't see what's so good about it." I have learned that everything is not as usual. The point here is that whenever we act, the response to our actions gives us information about the social system that we are in. That response may confirm some of our own thinking (frames and inferences) about the social system or it may provide some disconfirming data or as is often the case, it may do both. I may choose to follow up on Larson's comment and inquire further and try to understand what is up with Larson and how that might affect all of the interactions in the office this morning. Or I might choose not to because I have many other things to do today. Clearly I can't follow up and pursue the results of every action, I have to make choices. But

---

[2] One need only to read research papers from experimental psychology to see what sort of lengths one needs to go to do techno-rational sorts of experiment about the social world.

[3] This is the philosophical position of Action Inquiry (Foster 2013; Torbert 1991; Torbert and Associates 2004).

what I can do is make choices to actively experiment around those interactions that don't go as well as I'd like.

Planning Experiments

The first step in planning experiments is to understand how you make
sense of the interaction. That is, you need to analyze the interaction to
see how your own frames and inferences have led you to act in the way
you did and how that may have contributed to the situation. The tools
discussed in the previous chapters (the Ladder of Inference, the Learning
Pathways Grid, and the Change Immunity Map) can be very helpful to
get insight into how you make sense of things. This insight is the foundation of a hypothesis about the problematic interaction. The hypothesis
is that in a particular situation, you have a set of frames that lead you
to act in a particular way which contributes to the problematic results.
This is only a working theory and could prove to be wrong in a variety of
ways. However, it could also prove to be right, thus the need to conduct
experiments.

Let's look at an example. Sam[4] reflected on several problematic interactions at work where he felt like he was avoiding conflict. He avoided
giving difficult feedback to the people who worked for him, and he
avoided speaking up at meetings when he disagreed with the majority.
His analysis told him that he was avoiding conflict because he thought
direct conflict would make others dislike him and being liked by others
was very important to him.[5] Based upon his analysis, he formulated the
hypothesis presented in Table 5.1.

The next step is to create a basis for acting differently, in Learning
Pathways Grid terms, a set of desired frames and desired actions that he
could believe in and enact in the problematic contexts. In this case, Sam

---

[4] Sam is a pseudonym, and the example is a composite of a couple of different
experiments conducted by former students that had very similar issues.
[5] Part of his analysis was an application of developmental theory, and he identified
himself as being at the "socialized mind" (Kegan and Lahey 2009) or "diplomat"
(Torbert and Associates 2004) stage of development in which your actions are
very strongly influenced by what you believe others want you to do. There is a
lengthier discussion of developmental theory in Chapter 7.

Table 5.1 Sam's hypothesis

Context	Frames	Actions	Outcomes
When I disagree with the majority Having negative feedback to give to direct reports	Providing negative feedback to a direct report will cause them to dislike me as a supervisor Providing a dissenting opinion in a meeting will cause colleagues to dislike me Openly debating a request from my boss will cause him to dislike me	I avoid doing things that might jeopardize my popularity with others I find alternative ways to do these things that I believe are less apt to jeopardize my popularity	I avoid *ruffling feathers* I create extra work for myself and others as I seek out less confrontational ways to do things. I neglect some of my true responsibility as a manager. Others may recognize my inability to *stand alone* as a weakness in my leadership ability.

emphasizes frames that he cognitively believes to be true. He really does believe that it is acceptable and expected to share his opinion when it is contrary to the majority. He believes that his organization expects that from him even though he hasn't been doing that. He also believes, based upon a great deal of personal experience that his colleagues will not dislike him just because he disagrees with them about something. And finally he believes that part of his job as a manager is to provide negative feedback to the people who report to him so they can learn and develop. In the CIM terms, these are all column one commitments that Sam has been having trouble enacting (Table 5.2).

Of course, Sam believed in these new frames and wasn't able to enact them in the past, so simply identifying the new frames that he wants to enact isn't likely to be enough. Our big assumptions and the problematic frames identified in his hypothesis have a powerful hold on us, and we can easily find them controlling our behavior, even when we have done the analysis and know exactly how problematic they are. In addition to identifying a more desirable way of acting in the problematic situation, Sam's chances of actually being able to act differently and learn from the experiments are better if he also identifies specific situations in which to experiment, cues or triggers that will alert him to act differently, specific

Table 5.2 Sam's planned approach

Context	New frames	New actions	New outcomes
When I disagree with the majority Having negative feedback to give to direct reports	It is acceptable and expected that I share my opinion on different situations and decisions (even if it is contrary to the majority) Others will like me for who I am, not for whether I agree with them or not Direct reports expect and want me to share feedback, both positive and negative, in order to help them develop.	Openly express my opinion in meetings Provide direct reports and others with feedback that can help them to develop without concern for how it might affect their perception of me	I will be able to demonstrate the competency of *standing alone* Others will gain the benefit of my true opinion and the unique perspective that I can bring to discussions My direct reports will receive the benefit of honest feedback to help guide their development

phrases and words with which to enact his new actions, and possible outcomes of the experiment.

We can think of specific situations in which to experiment as designated practice fields. When working on any new craft or skill, we tend to start in a practice space—such as the practice field in sports or the rehearsal studio in theater. A good practice field allows you to experience some aspects of the game condition without the full pressure of having to perform when it really counts. It is a place where you can and are expected to make mistakes. When it comes to problematic situations, a good practice field is a place where the problematic dynamic is likely to come up, but the stakes are not too high. It is a place where if it turns out that your big assumption is correct and the worst thing imaginable happens, the pain won't be too horrible. A practice field may be a physical place, such as the office or home, or it may be a relationship, such as with your partner or trusted colleague, or even an event, such as a particular meeting. The key point is the combination of a strong likelihood of your own problematic behavior occurring and feeling safe enough to experiment with new behaviors. Sam identified a series of one-on-one meetings with his direct reports as a good practice field. The one-on-one meetings felt safer than acting in front of others and the stated purpose of the meeting which was to review the employees progress, reminded Sam of his commitment as a good manager to provide both positive and negative feedback.

The second part of a good plan is cues or triggers, which will alert you to act differently. We are often surprised when a problematic interaction happens and we find ourselves reacting rather than acting according to our plan. Our deeply ingrained habits take over and we do exactly what we always have done—we feel attacked and we counter attack, we feel that things are going badly and we try to take control to make them go better, the caller on the phone doesn't identify herself and I panic like a little boy failing a test. The most common cue or trigger to act differently is to be aware of and on the lookout for your own emotional response. How does it feel when the situation arises in which you wish to act differently? For Sam, the feeling when he doesn't speak up or give his direct reports negative feedback is fear. It's a particular type of fear that he recognizes as the fear of the shame of being excluded by others. He can feel it in the pit of his stomach, and he can easily mistake it for indigestion. But if he pays attention to it, he can tell the difference and that feeling is a trigger that tells him to think about what he is doing and act differently. Of course, his first response to telling himself to act differently is for the fear to increase. His analysis allows him to tell himself that the increase in fear is a good sign rather than giving in to it. His awareness of the fear or feeling of indigestion as a trigger allows him to pay attention to what he is experiencing and choose how to react rather than reacting unconsciously in his habitual way.

An alternative form of trigger is to force the issue and consciously choose to enter into a situation where the problematic behavior would typically appear. Rather than waiting for the interaction to happen naturally, you can make it happen. Sam can choose to meet with the people who work for him with the express purpose of providing negative feedback. The thought of doing this will almost certainly provoke his fear response. The advantage of forcing the issue is that you can take whatever time you need to prepare yourself. If you need to spend 10 minutes meditating to calm yourself before the interaction, you can do that. If you need to do it first thing in the morning when you have the most energy, you can do that. A final form of trigger is to ask for someone else's help. Perhaps your partner or a trusted co-worker can be enlisted to tell you when you are falling into a habitual and problematic behavior. It can be as simple as asking them to say, "Hey, you're doing it again" when they see you doing it. And even though it may be difficult for us to be aware of our own behavior, we are very good at seeing others' behavior and noticing what they are doing. The bottom line here is that you need some specific and concrete way of becoming aware that it is time to act differently. You need a trigger or cue to break out of your habitual behavior and experiment with new behavior.

The third part of a good plan is specific phrases that you can use. It is difficult to translate an intended action into speech in the heat of the moment, and there is a strong tendency for your old habitual frames to shape what you say, even when you have the best of intentions to act differently. For example, let's suppose you have a strong tendency to counter attack whenever you feel that you have been attacked. This is problematic because you have often jumped to a conclusion and are acting based upon incorrect assumptions about the other persons' intent so you decide that you will inquire first—you will seek first to understand and only when you are sure you have understood what the other is really talking about, will you respond (perhaps with a withering counter attack if appropriate, after all they may really be attacking you). So, when you feel attacked, you ask a question instead of blasting the other person. You say, "Why are you being such a jerk?" Of course, it's not a real question and your habitual frames have simply taken your stated commitment to inquire and used that as a new way to counter attack. The point here is again that our old frames are powerful and given the chance—even with the very best of intentions to do otherwise—it is very easy to fall back into acting from them. Having thought about what specific words you might use to enact your new frames can help tremendously in being able to actually enact those new frames in the heat of the moment.

In Sam's case, he looked to how his colleagues brought up dissenting opinions in meetings. Some did it well and others didn't. Those who did it well often started by saying, "I respectfully disagree ..." which indicated that they weren't about to make a personal attack. The actual

words and how they are said is critical. The similar phrase, "no disrespect, but ..." is often used in modern American popular culture and
is almost always followed by a personal attack and a great deal of disrespect. The difference is that the phrase, "I respectfully disagree ..." can
leave the focus on the issue, while the phrase, "no disrespect, but ..."
tends to shift the focus to the person. Of course, we have probably all
heard politicians use the phrase "I respectfully disagree ..." to suggest
that the other person is an idiot of the first order, so having the intent
to actually respectfully disagree and focus on the issue rather than the
person is an important part of the plan. The two phrases are similar, but
can have very different impacts, which is why you want to craft specific phrases that you can use. Role-playing the potential phrases with
friends can help you figure out what words to use and build up some
muscle memory for using the phrases in your experiment. Over time
the phrases can become part of you and you use them naturally, without
any conscious thought.

Most management skills include a set of stock phrases. When I first
learned the technique of active listening,[6] we practiced saying, "what I
hear you saying is ...." Over time we internalize these phrases and make
them our own. When I was first learning the skills of reflective practice,
Diana Smith taught us to say, "I know this probably says more about me
than it does about you ..." before we stated our inferences about others.
I seldom use those exact words, but the spirit of that phrase expresses
itself often when I speak. The phrases can feel awkward and inauthentic
when we first use them. But they can also serve as a crutch and give us a
way of starting to act differently when we are not very confident in how
we might do that. The specific phrases that you will craft depend on your
specific circumstances, but they can be informed by the wealth of interpersonal "how-to" approaches that exist.

The final part of a plan is some consideration of what might happen.
How will you know whether your experiment is a success? What do you
think you will learn? As a starting point, it is useful to think about what
reaction you expect from other people you will interact with. There is

---

[6] One of the more persistent and useful interpersonal skills (Rogers and Farson
1955)

probably a spectrum of potential responses from positive (which you are likely to consider successful results) to negative (which you are likely to experience as unsuccessful results). You should also consider how you expect to feel when you act differently. For example, if your analysis shows you that the primary issue is with how you are making sense of the situation such as in the example in the second chapter with my mother-in-law and answering the phone, I might expect to not be angry if I frame her actions as loving rather than rude. I might even expect to feel the love. More often, how I feel will be at least in part dependent upon how the other person reacts when I behave differently. So, it is useful to imagine two continuums of reactions from best case to worst case for both how you expect others will react and how you will react when you experiment with new behavior.

As an example, let's look at Sam's planned experiment with providing negative feedback to his direct reports. In the best case, his direct report will be thankful for the honest feedback. In the worst case, his direct report could have a strong, negative, and very emotional reaction—getting very defensive and verbally striking back at Sam. Those are, of course, short-term reactions. In the longer term, his direct report's reaction could range from taking the feedback on board and developing into a better employee to ruining the relationship he has with them—Sam's fear of others disliking him. The immediate reaction might be negative, and the longer-term reaction might be more positive. Or vice versa. Sam's internal immediate reaction might be to feel very afraid and sick to his stomach or it might be to feel honest and competent and good about himself. His feelings might be very different in the longer term. It is useful to recognize that the short-term immediate results may be very different than the long-term results. Thinking about all of these possibilities helps prepare Sam for what might happen. And indeed when Sam conducts his experiments, he gets a variety of results. One of his direct reports is actually thankful—a best case result. Another has a strong emotional reaction and gets very defensive. Sam's internal feeling is strongly affected and he feels good when his direct report is thankful and feels very stressed and unable to deal with it when his direct report gets defensive. But more on that in a moment.

Conducting Experiments and Paying Attention

With a good plan in place, you might think that conducting an experiment with your own practice of interacting with humans is pretty straight forward. You just go on with your life, and when the moment you have planned for arises, you notice it and act differently. Well, in some ways it is that simple. But in most ways it is anything but simple. Experimenting with your own practice requires a type of attention that most of us don't have. It requires that we are fully engaged in the moment, acting and interacting with others in the usual way, while at the same time watching ourselves interact with a sort of engaged detachment. This is not a description of multitasking because it's not about doing two different things at once; rather it is about doing one thing in two different ways at the same time. I'm tempted to suggest that it is easier to do than it is to describe, but that's not the case—it is difficult, particularly in emotionally demanding interactions.

In its most general sense, this ability to pay attention to multiple things at the same time is at the heart of mastering any craft. The craft master learns to simultaneously engage in their discipline and watch themselves engage at the same time. The woodworker works the wood and is consciously aware of how they are working the wood at the same time with a sort of engaged detachment. Early in your practice of a craft you learn to focus and the engagement is very attached to what you are doing. You need a master, or at least some skilled others, to watch you and give you feedback. You can reflect on your own action and bring that learning back into your practice in cycles of analysis, planning, and experimentation. As you progress in your craft mastery you learn to broaden your focus to be able to both engage in the process and watch yourself at the same time. Watching yourself allows you to judge what you are doing and make adjustments, in short to learn, to analyze what is happening and try something else if the current approach isn't working. This ability to watch yourself is at the heart of reflection in action,[7] which is the ability to learn and adjust your behaviors in real-time (rather than through cycles of offline reflection, analysis, planning, and experimentation).

---

[7] The terms reflection *on* action and reflection *in* action come from Schön's (1983, 1987) foundational work on reflective practice.

Paying Attention to Content

We can think about attention in terms of what we pay attention to. In terms of the Ladder of Inference, there is that great big pool of data which is far too big for any of us to be able to pay attention to all of it. So we choose—usually subconsciously—what we pay attention to and what we don't pay attention to. The key for experimenting is to make those choices more consciously and with the experimentation in mind. A starting place would be to think about paying attention to both the content and the process when you are experimenting. Of course, we all do pay attention to both to some degree, but what I am suggesting is that we be much more explicit about how we are doing that. Paying attention to content in a conversation is relatively straight forward and something we tend to do. After all, it is difficult to respond to what the other has said if we don't listen to what they are saying. But even here, it is not quite as straight forward as that because we often don't even listen to content very well. We often spend the time the other person is talking thinking about what we will say next and don't really listen to what they are saying much at all. Or it may take some time for whatever the other person has said to sink in and we won't understand what they have said until we each have said a couple of more things. Often we may be responding to what they said three utterances ago, or what we think we might have heard them say or even simply what we expected them to say. Paying attention to content means really listening to what people say and trying to understand what they mean. It requires a great deal of effort to do it well.

Paying Attention to Process

We all also pay attention to the process in some way. We tend to be particularly aware of the process when our expectation or desire for it to function in a particular way doesn't happen. We may have been looking forward to a dialogue on a topic, and when the other person speaks at length and we don't get a chance to speak, we become aware of the process as we say to ourselves (or our friends later), "that wasn't a conversation, that was a speech." For the purpose of experimenting, paying attention to process means consciously paying attention to what is happening, to the dynamics, to the actions, to the verbs. We tend to feel the others' actions when we talk with them and they feel our actions, but that feeling is usually part of our subconscious processing of the interaction. To pay attention to the process means consciously naming each action to ourselves. It is usually easier to pay attention to something if we have an analytical framework to work from. In order to pay attention to the actions that are being taken during the conversation, it is easier to place actions into existing categories than it is to name each individual action from scratch.

So as a way of starting to develop the skill of paying attention to the process, we can practice putting people's action into one of four categories: framing, advocating, illustrating, or inquiring.[8] Analytically, the distinctions between framing, advocating, illustrating, and inquiring are clear. Here are the definitions:

> Framing refers to explicitly stating what the purpose is for the present occasion, what the dilemma is that you are trying to resolve, what assumptions you think are shared or not shared (but need to be tested out loud to be sure). This is the element of speaking most often missing from conversations and meetings. The leader or initiator assumes the others know and share the overall objective. Explicit framing (or reframing, if the conversation appears off-track) is useful precisely because the assumption of a shared frame is frequently untrue. When people have to guess at the frame, they frequently guess wrong and they often impute negative, manipulative motives (e.g., "What's he getting at?").
>
> Advocating refers to explicitly asserting an option, perception, feeling, or strategy for action in relatively abstract terms (e.g., "We've got to get shipments out faster"). Some people speak almost entirely in terms of advocacy; others rarely advocate at all. Either extreme—only advocating or never advocating—is likely to be relatively ineffective. For example, "Do you have an extra pen?" is not an explicit advocacy, but an inquiry. The person you

---

[8] The four categories of action come from Bill Torbert (Torbert and Associates 2004). He calls them the four types of speech and says that you will be more effective when you consciously include all four types of speech in your interactions with others.

are asking may truthfully say, "No" and turn away. On the other hand, if you say "I need a pen (advocacy). Do you have an extra one (inquiry)?" the other is more likely to say something like, "No, but there's a whole box in the secretary's office."

Illustrating involves telling a bit of a concrete story that puts meat on the bones of the advocacy and thereby orients and motivates others more clearly. Example: "We've got to get shipments out faster [advocacy]. Jake Tarn, our biggest client, has got a rush order of his own, and he needs our parts before the end of the week [illustration]." The illustration suggests an entirely different mission and strategy than might have been inferred from the advocacy alone.

Inquiring obviously involves questioning others, in order to learn something from them. In principle, it is the simplest thing in the world; in practice, one of the most difficult things in the world to do effectively. Why? One reason is that we often inquire rhetorically, as we just did. We don't give the other the opportunity to respond; or we suggest by our tone that we don't really want a TRUE answer. "How are you?" we say dozens of times each day, not really wanting to know. "You agree, don't you?" we say, making it clear what answer we want. A second reason why it is difficult to inquire effectively is that an inquiry is much less likely to be effective if it is not preceded by framing, advocacy, and illustration. Naked inquiry often causes the other to wonder what frame, advocacy, and illustration are implied and to respond carefully and defensively.[9]

However, in practice the distinctions between the four types of action are not always clear. We may combine actions in a single utterance. We may advocate for a particular framing. We may put forward an advocacy in the form of a question (to make it seem less aggressive). Nonetheless, it is a useful framework to practice paying attention to the process of the interactions you are part of.

---

[9] Quoted from *Action Inquiry: Interweaving Multiple Qualities of Attention for Timely Action* (Torbert and Taylor 2008), page 244.

Practicing Paying Attention

As with practicing any skill, it can be helpful to start with a simple subset of the skill and gradually build to the fuller and more complex skill. So here's the first exercise. The next time you are in a meeting, pick one person to track. Make a small scorecard with a column for each type of speech and each time your target person speaks, decide what the action was and mark it on your scorecard. At the end of the meeting, you will have some data about what your target person's typical pattern of action is. Perhaps they advocate frequently, but never inquire. Perhaps they illustrate and inquire, but seldom advocate. During the meeting, you will also be participating in your usual role, so this is asking you to do two things at once. It provides practice in paying attention to and naming action in a limited way and practice in having multiple aspects to your attention. When you feel like you are getting comfortable with tracking one person's actions, increase the complexity and track a second person's actions as well. Then start tracking everyone's actions, including your own. With practice you can become used to paying attention to both the content and the process of what is happening. This generally proves to give you a lot of insight into what is happening in any interaction and can be useful for taking action. The next step in the practice is to act in an intentional way. After you have collected data in a few meetings on your own typical patterns of action, you can intentionally try to change that pattern. For example, if you find that you inquire a lot, but seldom advocate, you could try to balance your levels of advocacy and inquiry. The general rule of thumb is that including all four types of speech, with relative balance between advocacy and inquiry tends to be more effective. But you can test that and see for yourself. You will find that paying attention to both the content of the meeting as you participate in your regular role, as well as paying attention to the actions as you categorize them, and trying to act differently than you usually do is not easy. You may well fail and forget to categorize others' actions as you concentrate on balancing your own advocacy and inquiry. You may lose track of the content for brief periods as you focus on categorizing someone's actions—was she framing or advocating there, and oh, by the way what did he say in response? It's hard. It takes practice. But you can practice anytime you interact with other people.

There are of course ways other than content and process to divide your attention. You could practice paying attention to what is happening both inside and outside of yourself—how are you feeling in the moment, and what is happening in the world outside of you. Almost any dichotomy can serve as a way to remind you of what you are paying attention to and what you are not paying attention to. A little reflection will tell you what you typically pay attention to in a given situation and thus what you typically don't pay attention to. You can follow the same sort of structure of increasing complexity as outlined previously in relation to content and process and the types of speech with almost any dichotomy of attention. The key elements are to notice what you typically don't pay attention to (the process or actions) and then use an analytic categorization (the four types of speech) to structure your attention in that area. Continue your normal attention, adding a small target in the area you typically don't pay attention to. Then gradually expand the target of your attention (from one person to the whole group including yourself). Finally, intentionally act based in the domain you are trying to expand your attention into (balancing advocacy and inquiry). So as an example, if you are typically good at paying attention to the outside world and relatively bad at paying attention to how you are feeling, you might start with an analytic categorization of how you are feeling. There are many different categorization schemes for feelings, so as a starting place you might simply think of feeling state in terms of strength of feeling and whether it is positive or negative.[10] Your target to track would be your own feeling state. Your scorecard could simply record how you are feeling on those two dimensions at regular intervals. As you get better at paying attention to your feeling state, you might expand your target by expanding your categorization scheme to include specific emotions, or you might expand your target to include your guesses of what you think others are feeling (if that is part of what you typically don't pay attention to). Finally, you could act based on your feeling state—perhaps doing something as seemingly simple as sharing your feeling state with others whenever it becomes particularly strong.

---

[10] The psychological literature on emotion typically measures emotion on valence and activation, going back to *The Measurement of Meaning* (Osgood, Suci, and Tannenbaum 1957).

Regardless of how you define the various areas that you could pay attention to, the point is to practice explicitly paying attention to multiple aspects of our reality at the same time. This is the critical meta-skill of experimentation.

An Example of Conducting Experiments

Let's now turn back to Sam and look at how he experiments with his issue around avoiding conflict. Sam decided to experiment with giving negative feedback to one of his direct reports, Edwin (Table 5.3). Sam describes the experiment: "To set the stage, Edwin had applied for a Product Specialist position in the marketing group. He interviewed and had just learned that they had decided to give the job to another employee. It was important for me to understand how he received the news so that I could assess if he might be discouraged enough to start looking for opportunities outside of the company. He is a good hard worker and was

Table 5.3 Sam's first experiment

What Sam thought and felt	What was said
I hope that he is taking this okay and not getting into a funk. I can't afford to have him distracted, and we (the company) can't afford to have him leave. That's to be expected. Is he just playing it off or is he truly okay? This type of attitude says a lot about him if it is genuine. Well that seems to confirm that he is likely content and not going to look elsewhere for now. I know there were a few things that Greg mentioned to me that kind of swayed him the other way. Even though this isn't a fun conversation, I have a responsibility to make sure he does. Yup—this is what I heard, but they also mentioned a failure to cite true examples versus just textbook knowledge. Edwin should know this as well.	Sam: Hey Edwin—I wanted to check in and see how you were doing with the marketing job news. Edwin: Well, of course I'm disappointed, but I understand. Greg explained to me that they really could have gone either way and that I was definitely well qualified for the job. He indicated that he just felt that Sandra brought a little different balance of skills to the job that would likely fill some of the gaps. Sam: Well it sounds like you are taking the news really well. That says a lot about you. Edwin: Thanks. As you mentioned when we talked about it before, you never know what exactly they might be looking for, and I was glad to hear that they felt I was well qualified.

His eagerness to learn what he can do better makes this easy.

Well I remember that thing from Dawn a while back. I felt it was trivial and decided not to share it with him. Maybe I should bring it up.

It is amazing how things can get misinterpreted. Edwin is right that this information can help him. I've done him a disservice by holding back.

This response will make it easy for me to provide him feedback in the future.

This situation was minor and doesn't really bear any weight on people's opinion of him.

He has a great point here. Wouldn't I have wanted someone to tell me?

I need to make sure I provide him feedback in the future—both good and bad.

Sam: Did you ask if there was anything that you could have done differently?

Edwin: Yes, Greg indicated that a few of the interviewers felt that I came off a bit like a professor.

Sam: That sounds like what I heard. I also heard that they felt like you gave examples from *text books* as opposed to from your own experiences.

Edwin: Greg didn't mention that, but thanks for sharing. I really appreciate the feedback so that I can learn and do better next time. Did you hear anything else?

Sam: Let me think. This wasn't in regards to your interview, but this one time Dawn mentioned to me that she was surprised at your response to Jenn for some help. She indicated that you told her to go talk to the operators on the line. Dawn didn't feel that was appropriate for Jenn to do as a marketing person. In the end you got the information to Jenn, so I never bothered bringing it up with you.

Edwin: I didn't know this. I was merely suggesting that Jenn could go to the operators if she needed the information quickly. I always intended to get it for her. Thanks for letting me know this. I will be more careful to explain myself clearly with them in the future.

Edwin: I really do appreciate this feedback.

Sam: Like I said, I didn't really think it was a big deal so I didn't bother sharing it before.

Edwin: That may be so, but this feedback can help me avoid that from happening again in the future.

Sam: Well knowing how eager you are to get this type of feedback, I will be sure to share from now on.

Edwin: Thanks

a very close second for this job opportunity. The hiring manager also provided me some feedback regarding why he didn't chose Edwin that I felt would be valuable for him to hear."

This experiment went well, as most but not all do. We get some clue from the left hand column of what Sam is paying attention to. He is clearly focused on enacting his plan of providing the negative feedback to Edwin. We see him reminding himself that it is his responsibility to do this—a reminder of his new frame that his direct reports want to hear both positive and negative feedback and that it is part of his job as a manager to provide it. Fortunately, he also hears some confirming evidence for this frame when Edwin tells Sam that he appreciates getting the feedback. Sam is also focusing his attention on how Edwin seems to be feeling, notice he wonders, "Is he just playing it off or is he truly okay?" His focus on the others' feelings is directly related to his original fear that his direct reports would not like him if he gave them negative feedback. The data he really needs is how the other person is feeling. It is the data that Sam fears, and it is also the evidence that disconfirms the big assumption that drives his conflict avoidance. So, for Sam his attention is focused on both his own actions—doing what he plans to do—and the feeling state of his direct report.

Not all experiments go as well as Sam's interaction with Edwin did. Let's look at Sam's experiment with another of his direct reports, Shirley (Table 5.4). Sam describes it: "So if Edwin is the direct report that is easiest for me to provide feedback to, Shirley is the most difficult. Shirley has actually broken down in tears when I have tried to provide her feedback in the past. Often times, I didn't even consider that the feedback I am providing is that negative, so I struggle to understand where her response comes from. It often results in me backing off and not even being able to truly provide the full feedback I was intending. This month, she got her highlights to me on time, but another employee reminded me that she failed to provide monthly statistics for the pilot line over the past several months that we had asked her to do some time ago. This employee deemed it important as we were trying to determine how to speed up product development and one way he believed that we could do that was by improving the iteration rate on pilot line trials. Without this data, we couldn't understand how quickly we were iterating between experiments

Table 5.4 Sam's second experiment

What Sam thought and felt	What was said
Okay we better get to it before we run out of time before my next meeting.	As is always the case with Shirley, the conversation started with a bunch of general pleasantries back and forth about what was going on which left less time for the feedback.
Let me share the "What happened?" from my perspective.	It is important to note that Shirley was in a very good mood throughout the conversation.
Uh-Oh. I am on the verge of an emotional response from Shirley. Let me try to bring it back to the three conversations. Perhaps, if I provide a bit more of the details from my "What happened?" side.	Sam: Before we run out of time, I wanted to talk to you about the pilot line run summary.
	Sam: Scott mentioned to me the other day that he hadn't seen the monthly summaries of pilot line runs for the past several months. He was interested in this to understand how quickly we are iterating on development projects.
Maybe it would help if I offer that it isn't really a big deal in my mind.	Shirley (mood has visibly changed for the worse): I thought that I just had to do that the one time last year when I summarized things for the year.
That didn't help any. She is getting defensive and that isn't going to help us work through this.	Sam: I thought we agreed that we should continue reporting that information monthly so that we can watch for any trends. Since I am usually aware of what is going on, I didn't notice that it wasn't being done, but Scott doesn't pay attention to the runs weekly, so he values this information.
Crap—I was worried that there wouldn't be enough time to start this discussion. This isn't how I wanted this to end.	Shirley (visibly frustrated): I can't keep track of all of the e-mails that fly around asking me for stuff. I'll work on this and get it next week.
I'm sorry that we got cut short during our meeting.	(Phone starts ringing for the phone conference that Sam had scheduled)
	Shirley: I'll let you get your call.
	(She rushes out of Sam's office)

(Continued)

Table 5.4 Sam's second experiment (Continued)

What Sam thought and felt	What was said
Okay—at least she understands. But why did she get so upset? This feels a bit defensive. Others are able to keep up with the e-mail traffic and deliver on requests. I don't want to push on the phone, at this point just show that you are concerned and that all is well.	Once I am finished with my conference call, I decide to call Shirley to follow up. Sam: Hey Shirley—Sorry about my conference call cutting our meeting short. Shirley: No problem. I knew that you had it scheduled. Sam: You seemed upset when you left my office. Is everything okay? Shirley: Yeah—I'm fine. There's just so much going on and I can't keep up with all of these little requests that people send in e-mails. Sam: I agree there's a lot going on and it is hard to keep up. This really isn't a big deal, but the information will be useful for us. Shirley: I get that and I'll have it for you next week. Sam: That would be great

on the pilot line. I scheduled a meeting to meet with Shirley so that I could bring this up with her."

Here again Sam's attention is focused on what he has to do and Shirley's emotional state. As he focuses on what he has to do, he keeps in mind an analytic approach to acting, the Three Conversations from the book *Difficult Conversations*,[11] as he reminds himself to focus on the "what happened" conversation. He is also focused on Shirley's emotional state as he notes that he is starting to get an emotional response from her and then notes that she is getting defensive. This confirms Sam's worst fears and he has difficulty responding. When he reflects on the interaction after the fact, he realizes that when Shirley started to have an emotional response he should have shifted to the "feelings" conversation (staying with the *Difficult Conversations*, Three Conversations framework) and directly addressed what was happening in the moment. Upon reflection, Sam also realized that even though Shirley's emotional reaction triggered his fear, it did not really confirm his assumption that she would stop liking him because he was offering negative feedback. In fact, he really didn't know what Shirley's defensiveness and emotional reaction was about or what it meant for their relationship. What Sam did learn from this was one of the edges of his own practice—he could be very freaked out and unable to respond in a useful way by another's negative emotional reaction. As scary as it was, Sam realized that he needed to work on being able to act in a useful way, something other than simply retreating when others had a negative emotional reaction.

So, as is typically the case with experimenting, the results of one experiment lead to another. When Sam got a positive response from Edwin, it gave him the courage to move on to what he knew was a more difficult experiment with Shirley. And the less than positive response with Shirley also taught him something. We often learn more from failures than from successes. But the successes give us the strength to push our own practice farther, so we need both. Sam learned that he needed to understand what

---

[11] This is an excellent book by Stone, Patton, and Heen (2000) in which they suggest that difficult conversations are composed of a "what happened" conversation, a "feelings" conversation, and an "identity" conversation, all at the same time.

Table 5.5 Sam's third experiment

What Sam thought and felt	What was said
Let me see if I can simply lay it out and provide the facts in my mind and how it makes me feel.	Sam: Hey Shirley—I wanted to spend some time discussing something. In my opinion, you have a tendency to get rather upset and emotional when I provide you feedback. I am concerned since your response switches my focus from discussing the problem and potential solutions to dealing with the emotional response.
This is a good start. She admits that this is happening, and she isn't upset yet.	
First, let me acknowledge that there isn't anything wrong with having strong feelings about the feedback.	Shirley: I can't deny that I can get quite upset when I receive negative feedback.
But now let's focus on how to figure out how to improve the situation. Also, am I a part of the reason she has the strong emotional response?	Sam: There is nothing wrong with being upset. But I want us to be able to focus our energies on solutions. How might we be able to do this? Do you feel that I am too critical of you? That I don't provide you with enough positive feedback? Do you need more time to process the information before we discuss it?
Good. At least we have something to try. But I have some concerns ….	
Well, we can try this. I'm concerned since she initially complained about too many e-mails, but it is best for me to try her suggestion first.	Shirley: I don't really know. I think that more time to process might help.
	Sam: I hate the idea of just dropping something like this on you and then walking away though. How might we do this?
	Shirley: Maybe if you could send me an e-mail a day or two before we discuss it? That would give me some time to think about it and mentally prepare.
	Sam: I would be willing to give that a try.

was happening with Shirley when he gave her negative feedback. So he decided to ask her. Here are the highlights of the conversation (Table 5.5).

Sam continues his focus on what he has to do and on Shirley's emotional state. Interestingly—and it's not unusual—focusing directly on the emotions leads to a less emotional conversation. Sam learns that avoiding the feelings that are happening in the room may well have been making them more of an issue. It's an important lesson and one that will be the foundation of many future experiments for Sam.

And finally, how do we know if Sam has conducted a good experiment, How do we address the question of quality? The first question is whether Sam really managed to enact his plan. Our old frames can be hard to ignore and they often rise up and control our behavior in surprising ways. In Sam's second experiment, when Shirley starts to have a strong negative emotional reaction, Sam's old frames come into play and his plan for using the three conversations goes out the door. But even when we fail to enact our plans, it can still be a quality experiment if we can learn from it, which Sam did. So the primary quality criteria for experiments, is a pragmatic one—did you learn and did you transform the situation into a less problematic one? And good learning often consists not in having answers, but in having deeper understanding and better questions.

Choosing When to Experiment

This work is based in a philosophical position that all action is inquiry and all inquiry is action and thus we are constantly experimenting. Although this is a reasonable position, explicitly approaching all of our actions as experiments would be exhausting. And not all of our interactions are problematic, thus even though they may be experiments, we generally don't need to do extensive analysis and planning. So how do we decide when to experiment, when to dive deep into the details of our behavior and plan out ways to act differently? Clearly, we start with problematic situations—cases of conflict (overt or covert) or a relationship that is not what you want it to be or some other form of dissatisfaction.

Given the amount of time and effort required to do good, detailed analysis of your own behavior as well as the emotional courage it often takes to experiment with new behaviors, the second suggestion is to work on what matters most to you. That can mean a couple of different things. What matters most may be the most important relationship(s) in your life, if they aren't working the way you need them to. Or it could mean looking for your own most problematic behavioral footprint. By behavioral footprint, I mean a pattern of action that seems to happen over and over again in your life. It has the "here we go again" feel to it. If you have the same sort of conflict in your life with a variety of different people, the odds are that you and your behavioral footprint play a significant role in creating that conflict.

For most of us, it doesn't take a great deal of reflection to realize what your key problematic behavioral footprints are. If we tend to avoid conflict at any cost, we know it. If we tend to always insist on getting our own way, we know it. If we tend to have to always be in charge, we know it. However, if you don't know what your problematic behavioral footprints are, the people close to you probably do. You can ask your family, your close friends and colleagues, and once you convince them that you really want to know, they will tell you. They may even have tried to tell you in the past.

When you have identified your issue, your problematic behavioral footprint or the relationship you want to work on, start with a concrete example. You don't have to record an actual interaction; you can reconstruct one from memory. It will almost certainly be different than an actual recording of the conversation, but it will capture enough about how you understand and make sense of the interaction to be a useful starting place. Then do some analysis (using the tools and techniques discussed in the previous chapters) and plan your experiments. Conduct your experiments and analyze the results. Plan more experiments. And so on until one day you find yourself reflecting in action and paying attention in multiple ways as a matter of habit. Then every action really will be an inquiry and every inquiry an action.

A Checklist for Experiments

1. Planning
   a. Do you have insight into how your own behavior contributes to the problematic dynamic?
   b. Have you identified a practice field?
   c. Have you identified a trigger?
   d. Do you have a plan of action?
   e. Do you have specific phrases to say?
2. Execution
   a. Have you identified the multiple areas that you will attend to?
   b. Do you have an analytic framework for the areas of attention that you typically don't pay attention to?

    c. Have you practiced paying attention to multiple areas at the same time?

    d. Have you considered the possible range of results?

3. Post experiment

    a. Did you manage to enact your plan?

    b. Did you notice any disconfirming data?

    c. What did you learn?

    d. How do these results change or refine your understanding of the interaction?

    e. What new experiments does this suggest?

CHAPTER 6

Taking the Lead: Intervening into Dynamics

There has been an idea in our approach so far that by changing how you understand a situation and by acting differently, you can resolve problematic situations. This turns out to be true in a surprisingly large numbers of cases, but it isn't always true. Sometimes we are not willing to change how we understand things, perhaps because it is a matter of our core values or beliefs. And sometime the other person really is being the jerk you thought they were being. In these cases, you may need to intervene directly into the dynamics of the interaction.

In one sense, it is simple to intervene into the dynamics of a situation. You first recognize what the dynamics are and then you do something to change them. Of course, both halves of that can be relatively difficult, so we'll start out by exploring interaction dynamics (the actual actions in our Learning Pathways Grid [LPG] analysis in Chapter 3) and how we might usefully map or describe these. Then, I'll offer a continuum of intervention techniques and discuss some of the common problems and pitfalls of these approaches. I'd like to say that I could also offer a sure-fire way to avoid the common problems and pitfalls, but I don't believe that one exists. Intervening is a swamp, and you generally find yourself having to deal with it when the alligators are the most active.

Seeing and Mapping Dynamics

When I speak of dynamics, I am talking about the pattern of actions that people take when they speak.[1] It can be difficult to see the actions because

---

[1] Seeing speech as actions comes from the work of the philosophers Austin (1962) and Searle (1969) and the theater director Stanislavski (1936) and only recently in organization studies (Taylor 2005; Taylor and Carboni 2008).

we tend to pay attention to the content of what people are saying; that is, we focus on what they say rather than what they are doing when they say it. However, we usually feel the action and unconsciously respond to it. This means that it is the actions—not the content—that drive the emotionality of an interaction. When someone says something that makes us angry, it is not because they said, "Your haircut looks like it was done by a five year old," it is because they insulted you.

Identifying the action when someone speaks has two inherent difficulties. The first is that naming the action is always one step away from the observable data and thus there is no guarantee that any two people will name the action the same way. How we name an action depends not only on what the person said, how they said it, and what context it was said in; but also on the person naming the action's frames. What you might name as *jokes*, I might name as *bullies*. What you might name as *belittles*, I might name as *tries to help*. This inherent ambiguity as to what action is being taken leads to the second difficulty which is that impact and intent[2] are often different. When you act, it may impact the other person in a way that is very different from what you intended. And the way someone's action impacts you may be very different from what they intended. Adding to this difficulty is our tendency to assume that whatever the impact upon us was, it was also that person's intent. So if we feel hurt by someone's statement, we tend to assume that they meant to hurt us. This tendency produces a lot of the difficulty and misunderstanding in human interactions and learning to be consciously aware of actions is the first step in overcoming those difficulties.

We can get better at seeing dynamics by practicing. Much like with the attention exercises in the previous chapter, you can choose to pay attention to and explicitly name actions in your day-to-day life. You can learn a lot by naming the actions as they happen in the next meeting you're in. This is essentially the same as naming the actual actions in the LPG (and all of the same rules apply), but now we're trying to do it in real time rather than based on a two column case description of the conversation. Try to use the most expressive verbs you can. Over

---

[2] This distinction between impact and intent comes from the excellent book *Difficult Conversations* (Stone, Patton, and Heen 2000).

time, you will get better at it, and you will start making finer and finer distinctions in naming the actions (Table 6.1). It may not really matter whether your boss is goading your co-worker or provoking them, but it can be fun to think about the difference. It is useful to practice naming actions between others as well as those that are being done to you and by you. After you name to yourself how an action being done to you feels, try to step away from that feeling and guess what that person might have intended the action to be. Try and make the most generous inference you can about their intentions—assume they are an intelligent person who only means the best for you. The difference between the two can be striking and seeing the action from both perspectives is a critical first step in being able to talk about it.

Once you can see the actions, the next step is to map the pattern of actions. Let's look at an example. Raisha and Sandeep are newlyweds, deeply in love, but also not really used to living with each other. Like many young couples, they fight from time to time. For our purposes, it's not important what the content of the fights are about, what is important is how they fight—what is the pattern of actions or the dynamic of the fight? And when we look at the dynamics, all of their fights look alike. They tend to start with Sandeep doing something that Raisha doesn't like (which could be anything from making a joke that she found hurtful rather than funny to failing to pick up the dry cleaning as promised). She confronts Sandeep about whatever has happened. Sandeep always seems surprised and tries to answer whatever accusation she has made by explaining why it's not a big deal. This only seems to make Raisha angrier and she yells at Sandeep, repeating and deepening her accusations of his wrong doing. Sandeep then falls back on logic and works very hard to stick to the facts of the situation, usually physically moving away from her as much as he can. The pattern continues with Raisha getting angrier and Sandeep becoming less and less able to deal with her anger until he physically leaves. Eventually after some time has passed, Sandeep returns and Raisha tearfully apologizes and all is well again.

I'm sure you have a theory about what is going on with Raisha and Sandeep and may have even picked a side. But the point here is not that it is either's fault but that it is the way they interact that is problematic.

So let's map that interaction. As a first step, what are the actions we see? Raisha sees it like this:

- I raise an issue.
- Sandeep dismisses my concerns.
- I tell Sandeep it's important.
- Sandeep retreats into his shell.
- I try to get Sandeep to open up.
- Sandeep physically leaves.

On the other side, Sandeep sees it like this:

- Raisha attacks me about something.
- I try to calm her down.
- Raisha attacks me more.
- I try to defuse the situation.
- Raisha attacks me again.
- I leave.

This highlights the difficulties with working with dynamics. Each person names the actions from their own perspective. Both Raisha and Sandeep name the actions in a way that makes their own behavior seem reasonable and the others' behavior seem wrong in some way. That is our natural first response (Figure 6.1).

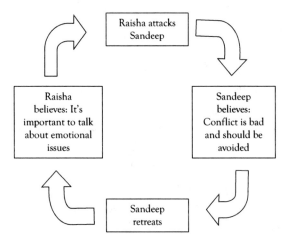

Figure 6.1 Raisha and Sandeep's dynamics

In order to map the dynamics, we need a mapping technique. Diana Smith[3] draws dynamics in terms of the actions of each party and the frames that lead them to act that way. Using her technique, we can draw the map of the interaction in Figure 6.1. Notice that we use the description of the action provided by the other person (just as we did with the LPG analysis in Chapter 3). This is because each person is reacting to the action they perceive, the action they feel. Also notice that given each of their frames, their actions are acts of pure genius. Raisha should keep pressing her case because she believes it is important to talk about emotional issues. Sandeep should run away from the conflict because he believes conflict is inherently bad. Which is not to say that these are conscious choices for either of them. In a very primal way, our fight or flight response is triggered whenever we feel attacked and given Sandeep's deeply rooted belief that conflict is bad, he has to flee—first by trying to defuse the situation, then by fleeing emotionally, and finally by fleeing physically. Raisha also has very little choice. For her, Sandeep's retreat is deeply insulting—how can he care so little about her that he isn't willing to talk about these things? For both of them, their frames come from their upbringing where they learned the *correct* way to handle negative emotions and conflict.

Focusing on the dynamics—without regard to the content—allows us to see the pattern of actions, and it is easy to see how this same pattern could happen around a variety of different subjects. We can also see that this pattern has a positive feedback loop in it. That is, the more Sandeep retreats, the more negative emotional energy Raisha will bring, which Sandeep will understand as greater and greater attacks, which will lead him to retreat more and more, until he finally he is out the door and Raisha is left fuming with anger at him. It's a negative spiral that can be very difficult to break out of. It's what Raisha and Sandeep mean when they tell us, "We only ever have the one fight. It's about different things, but it's the same fight."

The more general form of the dynamics mapping convention is shown in Figure 6.2. The diagonal line down the center of the figure highlights the different data that is available to each party. Each can see what the

---

[3] In her books *Divide or Conquer* (2008) and *The Elephant in the Room* (2011).

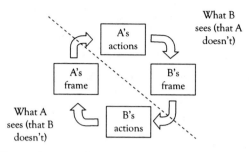

Figure 6.2 Dynamics mapping convention

other does and how they make sense of that, but they can't see what they do, nor how the other makes sense of it. This is another way of describing why problematic interactions can be so hard to resolve—it's as if each of us is seeing a completely different picture of what is happening in the interaction. Nonetheless, there is hope. Once we have a grasp of what is happening, we can intervene into the dynamics—recognizing that the emotionality, the anger, frustration, and so on of the interaction is usually directly tied to the pattern of actions.

Having identified the dynamics, the next step is to do something to change those dynamics into something more productive or less problematic—in short to intervene into the dynamics. There are three generic approaches[4] to intervening into dynamics, bypassing, naming, and engaging. Bypassing consists of simply acting differently and thus breaking the pattern. Naming interventions require explicitly naming the dynamics as a way to break the pattern. Engaging involves exploring the causes of the dynamics. In all three approaches, the intervention is designed to address the dynamics, not the instrumental content. Once the dynamics are addressed, then and only then can we move on to addressing the instrumental issue that seems to be at the heart of the conflict. We can place these interventions on a continuum from being less risky to more risky with bypassing being the least risky and engaging being the most risky. However, the same continuum could also be labeled from the least effective to the most effective for finding long-term solutions to reoccurring problematic interactions. So there is a trade-off and you will find

---

[4] This is primarily based in the work of Diana Smith (1995, 2008, 2011).

that the more difficult the interaction, the more risky your intervention will need to be. But this also suggests a way of working, first try bypassing, and if that doesn't work, then try naming, and if that doesn't work, finally try engaging. Let's look at each of these three approaches in more detail and consider how Raisha and Sandeep could intervene into their own dynamics to stop the fight.

Bypassing

Bypassing is conceptually simple. When you aware that you are enacting a well-established pattern of action, such as the pattern of Raisha attacking and Sandeep retreating, you simply do something—anything!—different than what you would normally do in that pattern. You can generally stay with the content of the interaction; that is, keep talking about the same thing, but you need to act differently. Of course, it is best to do something that has a good chance of getting the results you really want, but the key here is to break the normal, habitual pattern. For example, when Sandeep recognizes that they are in their "fight" dynamic, he could fight back rather than retreat. At first glance, it might seem counter-intuitive to fight back in order to stop a fight. However, this is the way it often works. A safari guide once told me that if a lion charged us, I should stand my ground (the first step in fighting back) because if I ran away, the lion would see me as food. After all, that was what the lion's food did—it tried to run away. Some of the faster prey might be able to get away, but I wasn't nearly fast enough. If I stood my ground, the lion would stop their charge 9 times out of 10 (I know—it's that 10th time that I'm worried about). In the same way, if Sandeep gives into the flight side of his fight or flight instinct, it makes Raisha mad and she continues fighting. If Sandeep can avoid fleeing (not just physically, but emotionally and cognitively as well), Raisha may well respond differently. And when Sandeep did fight back, that is, when he argued his side of the issue and expressed how he was feeling, Raisha did respond differently—she heard him and listened to what he was saying (at least 9 times out of 10).

As he was analyzing the interaction, Sandeep decided that he wanted do something other than the instinctual fight or flight. One of his inquiry group members suggested some emotional jujitsu, when he felt attacked by Raisha; he should hug her and tell her he loves her. It was not easy for Sandeep to respond to Raisha this way, but when he did, it was very effective at ending the "fight" dynamic. This idea of emotional jujitsu is based in a somewhat different understanding of the dynamics of the "fight." We could see the dynamic as being when Raisha expresses strong negative emotion and Sandeep reacts by trying to minimize the expression of strong negative emotion. In order to minimize the expression of strong negative emotion, Sandeep can counter the expression of negative emotion with a strong expression of positive emotion (hugging her and telling her he loves her) rather than trying to cognitively minimize the expression of negative emotion (by trying to minimize her concerns) or fleeing from the negative emotion. Raisha also has options for ending the dynamic. When she notices Sandeep retreating, she can back off and not "attack" him. She might also try some emotional jujitsu, and when she notices Sandeep retreating, she could tell him how much she loves him.

In order to be able to act differently, it is helpful for Sandeep or Raisha to understand their own frames, their own fears and identity issues, in short why they react the way they do. By using the tools discussed in earlier chapters, Raisha learned that she had a fear of being abandoned that was triggered by Sandeep's retreat. When he wouldn't meet her emotionally, she knew it was the first step in him leaving her forever. She could track this to specific events in her life and realizing that it was more about her past than about Sandeep helped her to be able to act differently. Sandeep also realized that he was afraid of being abandoned, but for him abandonment was preceded by being yelled at—by the expression of strong negative emotion. Realizing that this was more about him than it was about Raisha also helped Sandeep be able to act differently.

Of course, simply breaking the pattern of action doesn't resolve the issue. But it may resolve the negative emotional energy and create room for a different dynamic where the issue can be resolved. When Sandeep doesn't retreat, he and Raisha manage to talk about the issue. When he does retreat and Raisha responds by ratcheting up the level of emotional energy, the dynamic generates lots of emotion, but no communication.

Raisha and Sandeep's dynamic of attack and retreat is not uncommon. Some version of that dynamic often gets enacted by conflict avoidant people. The initial action may be felt as a request or a demand on their time rather than an attack, but for whatever reason the conflict avoidant person enacts their flight tendency by agreeing to whatever the other wants. And many people have the same response as Raisha when they interact with an extremely conflict avoidant person. They ask for something or suggest a course of action and when the other person agrees, they keep pushing because it feels like they are trying to push on water and they want to get the feel of something solid to push against. It is a frustrating interaction for both people and both can act differently to change it if they can recognize that they are enacting it.

Another common fight dynamic happens when a perceived attack is met with a counter attack—that is, when the fight response rather than the flight response kicks in. This can produce a very traditional fight, which can look like anything from a simple case of *butting heads*[5] to a full knock-down, drag-out fight. An analytic classification of action such as the four types of speech discussed in Chapter 5 can be helpful in identifying alternative actions. If the fight is best described as "I advocate my position, then he advocates his position, and then I advocate my position, and so on," then you might try including some inquiry as well as some framing and illustration. The ambiguity that is inherent in naming actions allows you to name any dynamic in a variety of ways. Different names suggest different ways of acting differently and different ways of bypassing the dynamic and creating a new pattern of action.

Naming

Sometimes bypassing a dynamic doesn't work. The dynamic can be so sticky, so attractive that all attempts to do something else fail to break out of the dynamic or lead into an even more problematic dynamic. Often we may think we're acting differently, but we're not really, we're just doing what we're doing in a more sophisticated way. For example, if I'm engaged in a battle of dueling advocacies, I may try to act differently and inquire. But if I'm really stuck in my frames, my inquiry may end up being a disguised advocacy, which the other person understands as advocacy and

---

[5] See, for example, our chapter on the LPG in the *Handbook of Action Research* (Rudolph, Taylor, and Foldy 2001; Rudolph, Taylor, and Foldy 2006).

the pattern continues. I may think I'm inquiring when I ask, "Why are you being such a jerk?", but I'm not. I'm really simply advocating my inference that the other person is being a jerk in the form of a question. In these cases, you may need to move to a more risky form of intervention—you may need to name the dynamic.

Naming the dynamic is about explicitly bringing the dynamic into the conversation. It is about shifting the focus (if only for a moment) from the content to the process; from the what to the how, the interaction is happening. Just like bypassing, the first step is to recognize the dynamic—to name it for yourself. However, if you want to have a successful naming intervention, how you name the dynamic is very important. Our first tendency is to name the dynamic based upon how it feels to us, which is probably very different than how the other person perceives it. Our initial naming of a problematic dynamic often implies a rather harsh negative judgment about the other. When Sandeep says that the dynamic starts when Raisha attacks him, he is implying that she has an intent to defeat him in some way. There may be other reasons to attack someone—hurt them, dominate them, put them in their place—but none of them feel very nice. So when Sandeep feels attacked, he knows that it implies something not very nice about Raisha and he does not want to name her action that way. Sandeep thinks it would not be good to say to Raisha, "don't attack me like that" or "why did you attack me?" He's probably right. It might change the focus from the content to the process, but it would probably do it in a less than helpful way.

Naming an action from your perspective is a way of sharing your feelings and constructive feedback techniques for doing that can be used. Classically, these techniques include a formula such as saying, "when you [describe behavior], I feel [name feelings]." Sandeep could say, "Raisha, when you say that, I feel like you are attacking me." The problem with this is that it takes a high degree of interpersonal skill for Raisha to hear the feedback in a way where she doesn't feel blamed. Often feedback like this can simply cause an argument about what the action is. Raisha responds by saying, "I wasn't attacking you," and we are off and running in a very pointless argument about what the one, single, definitive way to name her action is—and we know that there isn't a one, single, definitive way to name any action so that issue is not easily resolved.

A more useful way to approach naming a dynamic is to try and name the dynamic rather than naming either person's actions individually. That is, if you find yourself in a battle of dueling advocacies, you might say, "we seem to be butting heads here," rather than, "you seem to be strongly advocating your position without even considering what I have to say." It is often helpful to ask the other person if they are seeing the dynamic the same way. For example, you could say, "We seem to be butting heads here, does it feel like that to you as well?" By naming the dynamic rather than either individual's action, you are trying to move the point of view from your own perspective to the perspective of an outside observer. The question you have to ask yourself is, "how would a third party who was watching this describe it?" This is often not an easy question to answer and often our first answer to the question comes squarely from our own perspective. When Sandeep was asked to describe the dynamic from an outside perspective, he said, "it's like a boxing match where Raisha is trying to land haymakers to my head and I'm trying to play rope-a-dope and avoid her punches"; which is still clearly from his own perspective and names individual actions rather than giving a single name to the dynamic (both common problems when trying to name a dynamic). Sandeep, next created a more neutral description of the dynamic when he said, "we're doing that thing we do again." This actually proved to be a useful naming intervention because both Raisha and Sandeep knew what "that thing we do" is and yet it was ambiguous enough for both of them to not feel blamed in the naming of the dynamic.

There are a couple of key things to keep in mind when naming a dynamic in a naming intervention. First, try and pick less emotional verbs if you can. This is the exact opposite of how you named the actions for yourself when you were trying to understand them so there is a significant shift to be made. Less emotional names allow us to engage more cognitively and thus see our own dynamics with more distance and perspective. The second key is to try and name the dynamic as one thing rather than as a series of individual actions. Calling a dynamic a fight is better than saying "you hit me, and then I hit you back." Calling it one thing focuses us on that one thing rather than on the distractions of how to name individual actions. The third key is that ambiguity can be very helpful. An ambiguously named dynamic allows each person to connect to that name with their own felt sense of what it means. This creates space to explore the dynamic together and doesn't rush you into quickly assigning blame (something naming individual actions tends to do). So with these keys in mind, it can be helpful to have a few dynamic names in your back pocket. For example, I like *butting heads* because it feels like a fairly neutral description of a lot of different conflicts I find myself involved in. I also like *dance*, particularly when I am having trouble naming the dynamic more precisely. Almost all dynamics can be called a dance and perhaps the most generic naming intervention is something like "I hate it when we do this dance we're doing."

In naming the dynamic, not only do you move the focus from the content to the process, you are trying to make a fundamental shift from unilaterally taking responsibility for the interaction to fostering mutual responsibility. When using a bypassing intervention you are taking all of the responsibility for changing the dynamics of the interaction. When you name the dynamic, you are laying it out there and implicitly saying, "here it is, here's what we're doing, maybe we can do something else instead." You may wish to make some of that explicit in your naming intervention. The first step is to include an inquiry as to whether the other person sees the dynamic the same way and whether they think it is problematic. Although, in most cases if you feel an interaction is problematic, the other person will also feel it is problematic, that isn't always the case. You might find yourself saying, "It feels like we are butting heads here." The other person may respond, "Really, I felt like we are making some real progress on this issue—you know having good, spirited debate on the topic." In which case, you have learned something important. If the person agrees with you and says, "Yeah, we really are butting heads on this," you can take the next step and ask for their help in changing the dynamic. "Perhaps we can find a way to not butt heads?" This can lead to a tricky conversation because all of the same tendencies we had about naming actions to ourselves also exist when we have a conversation with others about actions and in real time it can be even harder to avoid emotional, judgmental descriptions of the actions. But it can also lead to a really great conversation. If you can stay curious and maintain an engaged detachment, it can be very useful to talk about how each of you perceive the dynamics and how you might be able to act in a way that would be more productive and feel better.

Naming a dynamic involves making the unseen seen. In that way it is somewhat like a work of art and not everyone will like it. Not everyone will agree that it accurately captures the essence of what was previously unseen. Like art, it is subjective and much is in the eye of the beholder. But also like art, over time there is often a surprisingly large amount of agreement when it is done well. Like art, when it is done well, it can open up our experience and life in surprising and unexpected ways. But sometimes, naming the dynamic is not enough to change it.

Engaging

Engaging a dynamic is a still more risky way to intervene. Engaging a dynamic means working with the other person to try and understand not only what you are doing, but also why you are doing it. Why do the two of you get stuck into this dynamic time after time? It's not easy to have a conversation about why the two of you enact a particular dynamic. It requires that both of you are willing to look at your own contributions and put your own fears and issues on the table for the other to see. It requires a great deal of trust and openness and perhaps above all, it requires high enough stakes to make the time spent worthwhile. Engaging a dynamic is a significant investment (in terms of time, emotional energy, and vulnerability) in the relationship, so it needs to be a relationship that is worth investing in.

Engaging a dynamic is generally best done at some time other than in the heat of the moment. Unlike bypassing interventions and even naming interventions, you generally wouldn't want to do it in the moment because it requires such a large commitment of time. When you ask someone to engage in a conversation about why the two of you fall into this pattern again and again, it is not going to be a short conversation. It is hard to imagine being able to have a useful conversation that takes less than an hour. And it is easy to imagine that the conversation might require multiple sessions—with time for personal reflection for both parties in between—to really resolve the issues. It is also useful to not do it in the heat of the moment because a good engaging conversation requires both parties to put aside their own emotional reactions and look at the dynamic from a more neutral point of view, which is really hard to do in the heat of the moment.

If you have recognized a problematic dynamic in your life and bypassing and naming interventions haven't worked for you, or if there is a *cold* conflict simmering in an important relationship in your life, it can be time to try an engaging intervention.[6] The generic steps are: (1) name the dynamic, (2) ask if they are willing to explore the issue with you, (3) listen to their understanding, (4) share your understanding, and (5) jointly construct new ways of understanding. None of these are simple and each step along the way tends to feel risky until we have gained a lot of personal skill in having these sorts of conversations. Of course, as you get better at having these conversations, most people tend to have less need to have them—they have fewer and fewer dynamics that get to the point of needing to be engaged, so there is something of a Catch-22[7] here. If engaging feels really risky or you lack confidence in your ability to have a productive conversation, you might want to try a variation of an engaging intervention in which you involve a neutral third party who acts as a mediator in the process. I call this the *couples therapy* option and it can be very helpful with the right person as mediator.

The first step is the most critical and as discussed earlier, it can be very difficult. How we name a dynamic matters a lot because of our tendency to name it based upon how it feels to us which often implicitly blames the other person. The same guidelines for naming the dynamic that were discussed in the previous section on naming interventions apply here. You should try and name the whole dynamic rather than each person's actions

---

[6] This approach draws heavily upon the *Difficult Conversations* (Stone, Patton, and Heen 2000) method.

[7] "There was only one catch and that was *Catch-22*, which specified that a concern for one's safety in the face of dangers that were real and immediate was the process of a rational mind. Orr was crazy and could be grounded. All he had to do was ask; and as soon as he did, he would no longer be crazy and would have to fly more missions. Orr would be crazy to fly more missions and sane if he didn't, but if he were sane he had to fly them. If he flew them he was crazy and didn't have to; but if he didn't want to he was sane and had to. Yossarian was moved very deeply by the absolute simplicity of this clause of Catch-22 and let out a respectful whistle." (Heller 1961, 56).

if possible and try and name it in as a neutral a way as possible. Ideally, you should name the dynamic the way a neutral third party who had seen it happen might describe it. Naming actions with evocative verbs was helpful when analyzing the interaction, but when naming it to the other party you should try to use the least evocative verbs possible. Since this is the first step in the naming intervention you can craft the words you want to say offline and even practice them with your inquiry group members or other friends. Our first attempts tend to still be from within our own frames regardless of how hard we try to find an outside perspective and other people can be extremely helpful in pointing that out.

Often the other person also has strong feelings about the problematic interaction, so they may not react well to your description of the dynamic. The odds are good that they do not see it the way you described it, but instead see it based upon how it felt to them. You should be prepared for them to name the dynamic in their own way and be persistent in your invitation to engage in a discussion about why the two of you fall into this pattern. For example, here's Raisha taking the first two steps (naming the dynamic and extending an invitation to jointly inquire into it) in an engaging intervention with Sandeep:

> Raisha: Sandeep, I'm really concerned about the fights we've been having. Could we talk about why we fight like this?
>
> Sandeep: You mean you wonder why you attack me like you do.
>
> Raisha: I get that that's what it feels like to you. Could we sit down and talk about what happens and why it happens that way. I think it would really help me.

With an engaging intervention, you need to be persistent and expect some sort of emotional reaction. You may need to give the other person some time to get ready—just because you are now ready to talk about the dynamic doesn't mean that they are. You can suggest a time and place—something relaxed over food or drinks can be good—for the conversation to take place so that they can be prepared as well. And in some cases, the other person just won't be interested in talking about it at all. You can try and convince them, but unless they are willing to engage, you can't successfully do this.

The second step is pretty straight forward; invite them to explore why you two enact the dynamic. You should be clear in your invitation that you don't necessarily mean right now. Something like, "would you be willing to have lunch one of these days and talk about why that happened, why we seem to continually do this, and how we might interact in a more productive way?" is good because it extends the invitation, makes it clear that you're not talking about doing it right now, and lays out what the agenda would be. You may need to follow up the invitation with more detail about how you see the discussion unfolding. The emphasis should be on jointly seeking more mutual understanding and working together to find a different way of acting that works for both of you. It is not about you telling them what a jerk they were or them telling you what a jerk you were, although both of those topics may come up. And if there is a clear power differential, such as between you and your boss or you and one of your direct reports, you'll need to be especially careful in laying out the ground rules to minimize the effects of that power differential. If they agree, then it is on to the third step and having the conversation, which is steps three, four, and five.

It's best to start the conversation by listening to the other person's understanding of the dynamic. This can be difficult because their understanding is from their perspective, and from their perspective, it probably feels like the whole thing is your fault. None of us like to be blamed—particularly when we feel it isn't fair—so you have to prepare yourself for hearing it. The critical thing is to really listen and try to understand. You need to have as much empathy for them as you can and approach the conversation with an almost insatiable curiosity. Techniques such as active listening can be helpful to make sure that you really understand their experience of your interaction. You may be tempted to try and "fix" their understanding or correct what seem like basic factual errors, but try to avoid doing that. One of the key insights that the *Difficult Conversations*[8] approach provides is that people generally cannot hear your story until they have told their story. Of course, the opposite is also true, and you may have difficulty hearing their story before you have told your story. This impasse can only be overcome if someone goes first and listens before

---

[8] From the book of the same name by Stone, Patton, and Heen (2000).

they have told their story. It's your job to be that someone. There is also a therapeutic value to having someone listen to your story and simply listening empathetically can go a long way toward making the other person feel better about your relationship.

Once the other person has shared their story of what happened, it's your turn to share your story. You should try and focus on what is really important to you and take responsibility for your actions and your contribution to the dynamic. This is your opportunity to open your heart to the other person and build on the positive feelings that have come from listening empathetically. It is not about apologizing, although that may be part of sharing your own story if you feel it is appropriate. This is an opportunity to share all of the insight you have gained from using the various analytic tools such as the Ladder of Inference, LPG, and Change Immunity Map. You may feel very vulnerable when you admit your culpability to the other person, but the vast majority of the time that vulnerability is rewarded with mutual sharing and increased connection in the relationship. Your sharing may inspire additional sharing by the other person. It is remarkable how hearing someone else admit that they aren't perfect and that they acted in a way that they are not very proud of, can free us to admit the same about our own behavior. If the conversation goes well, there may be a fair amount of back and forth with deeper and deeper sharing. Just as with the invitation to engage in a discussion of the dynamic, it may be useful to allow some time for processing between rounds of sharing and between sharing your stories and crafting alternative ways of being. Exactly how much to share, how many times to go back and forth and when to move toward constructing new ways of understanding is based entirely on the specifics of how the situation goes and every engaging conversation is unique.

The final step is to work together to craft a different way of interacting. This may flow naturally from sharing each other's stories or it may require an explicit move to talk about how each of you can reframe and behave differently. It can be very powerful to make some commitments to each other and to ask each other for help in behaving differently. For example, Raisha and Sandeep agreed that as a first step, when either of them became aware that they had fallen into their fight dynamic, they would simply name it and ask for a time out. Raisha admitted to Sandeep that when she felt like he was running away from her, she got really angry because it raised a whole host of abandonment issues she had and if he could hug her in that moment; it gave her the strength to get past the anger. Sandeep admitted to Raisha that he often didn't realize he felt attacked, and that his retreating behavior was pure instinct, and if Raisha could name what he was doing without a lot of emotion he could more easily engage with her on whatever the issue was. These agreements gave both of them a way to help the other and shared the responsibility for breaking out of the old destructive, dynamic.

Engaging a dynamic can feel a lot like you are asking the other person to engage in a mutual therapy session. And the engaging conversation can feel like a therapy session. On the plus side, a good engaging conversation can go a long way toward improving a relationship and making you feel closer and more connected to the other person.

Becoming a Conflict Whisperer

Analyzing the dynamics of an interaction and experimenting with bypassing, naming, or even engaging interventions is another technique that you can use as you work on mastering the craft of interacting with other humans. I have been avoiding including the actual words people are saying in order to keep the focus on the actions and not the content. Although trained actors can enact almost any action with almost any line, most of us are not that skilled at letting our consciously intended action shine through. So, it is critically important to craft actual words you will say and try them out with other people to see if it feels like the action you intend. This is a step in learning to see not just others' actions, but also to start to recognize how your actions might be perceived by others.

Learning to see dynamics in real time is the first step in becoming a conflict whisperer, someone who can almost magically nip conflict in the bud and stop fights before they cause lasting damage. The great insight of the Russian theater director Stanislavski was that actors can produce authentic behavior on stage by focusing on the action—not the emotion, or the content. Actions are what we do to each other and seeing actions allows us to understand what is happening rather than what is being discussed or who is feeling what.

Although bypassing interventions can be very powerful and can resolve a conflict by enacting a different and non-conflict-based dynamic, they can also serve to hide or delay the underlying issues. Your real power as a conflict whisperer comes when you learn to name dynamics in ways that don't blame those involved. This only comes with practice, but when you become skilled at it, you are able to enact a series of moves that are at the heart of resolving conflicts. Once you have named the dynamic, you can ask other people for help in enacting a different dynamic. You can also own your own contribution to the dynamic and admit it to the others involved. Seeing others take responsibility for their contribution often opens the door to allow us to also admit to our contribution.

We can learn to see dynamics with practice. But in order to learn to name dynamics from an outside perspective, we must be curious. We must have a fundamental stance of curiosity about how we are interacting with others. It is based in the same sort of attentional quality that I earlier described as engaged detachment. As you interact with someone, you can be constantly asking yourself, what are we doing? What is the dynamic here? Holding that sort of curiosity is not easy and I will spend a considerable amount of time suggesting why it is so difficult in the next chapter. However, it is essential for becoming a conflict whisperer.

Table 6.1 A useful list of verbs for naming behaviors

abase	charm	dramatize	induce	promote	soothe
abolish	chastise	draw	indulge	prompt	spellbind
absolve	cheat	duck	insinuate	propel	spoil
abuse	check	ease	inspire	propose	spur
accept	cheer	educate	insult	propound	spurn
acquaint	chide	elevate	intrigue	prosecute	squash
acquit	clarify	embroil	invite	provoke	squelch
addle	coax	enchant	judge	pursue	startle
address	coddle	endear	lambast	quash	still
admonish	coerce	endure	lampoon	quench	stir
affirm	collude	engross	lecture	rack	stretch
afflict	command	enkindle	liberate	rally	strike
affront	commend	enlighten	lure	ratify	strip
aid	conceal	ensnare	magnetize	ravage	study
alarm	condemn	entangle	malign	rave	stymie
alert	confide	entertain	maneuver	rebuke	suffer
allow	confirm	entice	mask	recreate	suggest
allure	confound	entrap	mend	rectify	summon
amaze	confuse	entreat	mimic	reiterate	supplicate
amuse	contest	eradicate	mislead	reject	support
anger	convince	estimate	misuse	rejoin	suppress
anticipate	correct	evade	mobilize	release	surprise
approach	court	evaluate	mortify	relegate	swindle
arouse	criticize	excuse	motivate	remedy	tantalize
arrange	crucify	exploit	muffle	renege	tarnish
assist	crush	facilitate	mystify	repel	tease
astound	curse	feed	nag	repress	tempt
attack	damn	force	nauseate	reprimand	terrify
baby	dare	frame	negotiate	repulse	thwart
badger	deceive	free	notify	resist	tickle
baffle	deduce	frighten	nullify	retract	titillate
bait	defy	frustrate	obliterate	revolt	tolerate
bear	delight	fuddle	offend	ridicule	torment
beckon	delude	gag	oppose	sanctify	torture
befuddle	demean	gauge	organize	satisfy	trick
beg	denigrate	gladden	orient	scheme	trouble
beguile	deny	goad	overlook	scold	tyrannize
belittle	deter	hallow	panic	scrutinize	unburden
berate	devastate	harangue	patronize	sedate	uproot
bewitch	dictate	hassle	perform	seduce	urge
bid	direct	help	perplex	settle	vacillate
blame	disconcert	hoodwink	persecute	shake	validate
bless	discredit	humble	peruse	shame	verify
bluff	disgrace	humiliate	placate	shroud	victimize
boost	disgust	humor	please	shun	vilify
brainwash	dishearten	hurt	pledge	sicken	vindicate
bribe	dispirit	hush	pose	slander	warn
catch	dissuade	hypnotize	pray	slur	wheedle
caution	divert	imitate	press	smother	woo
censure	divine	impair	prick	snare	worry
challenge	dodge	implicate	prod	sober	worship
charge	dominate	indict	promise	somber	wrangle

CHAPTER 7

The Leadership Journey: Being Curious

So far, I have been focusing on the tools that you can use to master the craft of interacting with others. You may have noticed that using the tools implies a certain shift in how you approach interacting with others. The simplest way for me to describe this shift is from knowing to curiosity. By knowing, I mean the sort of certainty that we humans have about what is happening in interactions with others, the way in which we think we know what others and ourselves mean as we interact. However, as the various tools we have explored so far have shown us, we are often wrong about what we know—about both others and ourselves. We are also often right. However, we tend to be overconfident about just how right we are, and because it is easier to work from our own frames and inferences than to actively test those frames and inferences. But we are wrong more often than we think we are. The shift to curiosity is a shift that requires you to work harder in your interactions with others, to pay more attention to what is going on, and to have a lot more humility around what you know. It means holding your inferences lightly and testing your own frames—actively looking for evidence that contradicts and disconfirms your deeply held assumptions about the world. It's not easy.

This shift is talked about in various ways by various theorists. The book, *Difficult Conversations*[1] describes it as a shift from a *battle of messages* to a *learning conversation*. The *battle of messages* is based on a confidence about our own knowing—we're right, the other is therefore wrong and it is our job to convince them of our position. The learning conversation is based on curiosity—how does the other understand things, why do they make sense of things that way, how do they feel about the

---

[1] By Stone, Patton, and Heen (2000).

situation? In my terms, how are their actions acts of pure genius? Interestingly, being curious is also at the heart of the craft of artistic processes. The master craftsperson is always curious about new and different ways to do things. What if I try it like this, what happens then? If you have a craft skill (whether that is glass blowing, playing an instrument, hitting a golf ball, or playing a particular video game) you may have developed something of this stance of being curious as part of your practice of that skill. And although it may seem like a simple thing to bring that curiosity to our own interactions, to take what you know in one part of your life and apply it in another part of your life, it usually isn't easy for reasons, which we shall get into shortly.

Staying with Your Senses and Not Knowing

In order to get more of a feel for what I mean by being curious, let's look at it in terms of craft mastery and artistry. Artists often refer to the state as being open. Open to their art, open to the possibilities, open to the emerging reality, and open to the journey. I characterize this[2] openness as the combination of staying with your senses and a willingness to not know. Staying with your senses[3] means fighting against our tendency to quickly make sense of our world, and then work from that sensemaking, rather than continuing to pay attention to the evidence of our senses. To illustrate this tendency, try this exercise: Take a long look in the mirror and then do a quick sketch of your own head. Now look at the sketch and answer the question: How far from the bottom of your head are your eyes? Are they half way between the top and bottom of your head? Are they two-thirds of the way up from the bottom of your head, or are they three-quarters of the way up? For most people the answer will be two thirds or even three quarters of the way up—even though the eyes are very close to exactly halfway up the head in humans. That's because you

---

[2] Initially in an editorial in *Organizational Aesthetics* (Taylor 2013b).

[3] I dedicate an entire chapter called the "Creative Mindset" to this in *Leadership Craft, Leadership Art* (Taylor 2012). Claus Springborg (2010, 2012) originated the phrase "staying with your senses." And prior to that, many artists expressed this idea, such as Betty Edward's (1979) in her well known book, *The New Drawing on the Right Side of the Brain*.

drew your sketch from your mental model of your head rather than from what you saw when you looked in the mirror. And that mental model puts more emphasis on your face (the area from your mouth to your eyes) than on your forehead because we get most of the important information from people's faces (and not from their forehead and hair). So our mental model makes the face bigger and the forehead smaller, so we draw our face bigger and the eyes get put farther up the head than they actually are. Craft mastery in drawing requires staying with your senses and really seeing what is out there. It means not getting lazy, but continuing to be curious about what you are actually seeing on an ongoing basis. It means not looking once, but continuing to look minute after minute. This is hard. But it is worth the effort. Try this exercise. Pick something really interesting to look at—I'd suggest a painting in a museum. Then sit down and look at it for three hours. Keep a paper and pencil handy and write down what happens over the course of the three hours. What do you notice at different times? How bored do you get? Do you want to kill yourself? What happens to your understanding of the painting over the three hours? How often did you drift off and stop really looking? By the end, at the very least, you will realize just how difficult it is to stay with your senses, and if you're like most of us, how seldom you habitually do so.

The flip side of staying with your senses is the ability to not know.[4] At its simplest, it is the motivation for staying with your senses—because if you don't know what is out there you can find the world an exciting and interesting place and you will want to discover all of the fascinating things about it. And if you already know, why bother to look? Once I know what my face looks like, why would I spend the effort to really look at it? But the idea of not knowing is more than that. It was expressed by the poet John Keats as, "Negative Capability, that is when man is capable of being in uncertainties, mysteries, doubts, without any irritable reaching after fact & reason."[5] Keats saw this as a critical ability for any artist. It is an ability to tolerate, perhaps even be comfortable with the ambiguity

---

[4] The phrase "not knowing" comes from the work of Ariane Berthoin Antal (2013).

[5] In a now famous letter to his brothers in December of 1818 (Keats 1970, 41–42).

that we all face in the world. For Keats it was not a short-term thing, not a "I don't know this right now, but I will figure it out" thing,[6] but rather a willingness to believe that there are fundamental mysteries that we will never know the answers to. For the artist, negative capability creates space where she can create new things. For the master craftsperson, being comfortable with not knowing creates a safe place from which to question your own practice.

One of the benefits of being curious, of staying with your senses and being okay with not knowing is the way in which it increases your empathy. Staying with your senses keeps you in the present and helps you connect with both yourself and others, which lays the groundwork for having more empathy, both for yourself and for others. Not knowing creates space for you to understand others in ways that are less harsh and judgmental (which is all too often our first instinct when we come from a position of knowing). That is, when we *know* what is going on, it usually means we know what the other is thinking and what motivates them. This thinking is based in our own felt sense and for difficult interactions that felt sense is usually negative. The impact of the others' action on us feels bad, so we know that they meant to make us feel bad and it is very difficult to have empathy for someone who means to make you feel bad. Not knowing requires setting aside our own immediate reaction, our own immediate rush up the Ladder of Inference. Staying with your senses requires you to actively pay attention to what is going on and look for evidence that contradicts or changes your initial understanding of the interaction. Being curious includes both.

The Problem of Mystery—Mastery

It is not easy to stay curious in our interactions with others. Craft masters learn to stay curious in regards to their craft, to be curious about how they are making music with others, about how they paint, or whatever their craft happens to be. But there is a difference between being open to your craft and being open when you interact with other people. And

---

[6] Which I might (somewhat flippantly) call engineering curiosity as opposed to artistic curiosity.

that difference is that being open when you interact with others makes us feel vulnerable, it opens up my sense of me and allows others to questions that. This is a problem because, for most of us, at some level we are our frames. We are the theories, assumptions, and beliefs that we hold about the world. That is what makes me, me. And when those frames are threatened or even just questioned, then my identity itself is questioned. Of course, not all of our frames are a foundational part of our identity, but the important ones—which are the ones that usually are causing the problems when we have difficult interactions with others—are part of our identity.

However, because we are all geniuses, the problem is even more difficult than that. We have created a culture in which we all learn a set of frames that prevents us from questioning our own identities. This set of frames was identified by Agryis and Schön[7] and they called it Model I. It consists of a set of four governing values:

- Achieve the purposes as the actor perceives them
- Maximize winning and minimize losing
- Minimize eliciting negative feelings
- Be rational and minimize emotionality

On the face of it, they look like a pretty reasonable set of values. And we might even think of them as a set of ideal values for polite society. If everyone just lived by those, we wouldn't have so many difficult conversations, right? And that is the genius of these values—they seem reasonable and at first blush we are all likely to agree to them. However, the really brilliant work that Argyris and Schön did was to show[8] how acting from these values prevents us from learning about our frames and thus protects our identity from being questioned.

It is perhaps easier to intuitively understand why these values are problematic and work to keep us in a state of knowing (rather than being curious) if we use Torbert's version of the same values. He calls the model

---

[7] Starting with their classic *Theory in Practice* (Argyris and Schön 1974).
[8] In detail that I won't reproduce here, but I encourage you to read the original work if you are at all inclined.

I values, "Mystery—Mastery"—the goal being to master the external world (including others) while keeping the internal world a mystery to others. We must keep our internal world a mystery to others so that it is not open to being questioned. We must master the external world in order to bend it to our will, in order to do whatever it is we want to do. In contrast to this, Torbert suggests adopting a stance of Collaborative Inquiry. This idea of Collaborative Inquiry looks a great deal like Argyris and Schön's Model II, which has the following governing values:

- Valid information
- Free and informed choice
- Internal commitment to the choice and constant monitoring of the implementation

And to some large degree, it doesn't matter whether we call it Model II, Collaborative Inquiry, being curious, or being open to the world—it is a way of being in the world that we are by and large not used to and find very difficult to enact on a consistent basis.

The Developmental Journey

We can also understand the shift from knowing to being curious as being a particular transition on our developmental journey through life. The idea that we develop in various ways as we grow older is accepted as common sense. We know that children go through well-defined stages in motor skills, speech, vision, and social development. What you may not know is that there are also stages of development that can (and often do) continue throughout our adult life.[9] Just as a child progresses through key stages such as being able to recognize that their toes are part of themselves to dropping things and watching where they go to being able to walk and so on, there is also a progression through different action-logics that drive how you make sense of the world. You can think of these action-logics as a set of frames that determine how we understand the world around us.

---

[9] For a fuller discussion of developmental theory, read *In Over Our Heads* (Kegan 1994) or *Action Inquiry* (Torbert and Associates 2004).

That's not to say that everyone follows an identical path in their development or sees the world exactly the same way—just as not all babies learn to walk in the same way or at the same time. It's useful to think of the stages of development as expanding our cognitive, emotional, and behavioral repertoire just as the stages of a child's physical development expands their repertoire of physical abilities. Within each stage, you still have all of the action-logics of the previous stages and there may well be times where those previous action-logics drive our behavior. In order to illustrate this developmental journey, I draw upon Edward Kelly's[10] analysis of the American billionaire, Warren Buffett's life.

The first action-logic that Kelly describes is the teenage Buffett as an Opportunist.[11] The Opportunist action-logic is about gratifying immediate needs, driven by the question—what is in this for me? Buffett undertook a variety of early business ventures, but also ran away from home and by his account didn't treat others particularly well. Buffett transitioned to the Diplomat action-logic in his later teenage and undergraduate years. Here the action-logic is driven by a need to belong—how do I fit in?— and social norms now rule over personal needs. Buffett isn't naturally good at this, so he reads Dale Carnegie's *How to Win Friends and Influence People*. After college, Buffett's action-logic shifts to the Expert stage as he adopts Graham's value investment approach. The action logic is driven by expertise and the craft logic now rules social norms. Buffett has success with the Expert action-logic, but his greatness comes in his thirties when he transitions to the Achiever action-logic and establishes the Buffett Partnership (which achieved a 24 percent average yearly return for over a decade). The Achiever action-logic is driven by goals and organizational effectiveness rules over the logic of the belief system.

These first four action-logics are referred to as conventional development and most of the people we encounter in our lives are acting from one of these stages of development.[12] There are a couple of things that are

---

[10] This comes from the first of a three part series of articles on the subject (Kelly 2013).

[11] Kelly follow's Torbert's naming convention for the developmental stages. Kegan uses somewhat different names.

[12] Rooke and Torbert (2005) found that roughly 85 percent of managers they tested measured at one of these first four levels using a sentence completion test instrument.

worth noticing about these stages. The first is that they correspond very closely to Argyris and Schön's Model I governing values.[13] The Opportunist action-logic is about maximizing winning and minimizing losing. The Diplomat action-logic is about minimizing eliciting negative feelings from others. The Expert action-logic is about being rational and minimizing emotionality. The Achiever action-logic is about achieving purposes as the actor perceives them. A common aspect to these action-logics is that the action-logic is an unquestioned (and largely unquestionable) part of our identity. We are the action-logic—thinking of them in terms of frames, we don't see the frame only the picture that is framed.

Looking at the transitions between action-logics, you can see that each action-logic solves a dilemma that is unsolvable in the previous action-logic. For example, the Opportunist is ruled by their personal needs. But being ruled by your personal needs can cause real problems when it comes to being part of a group. The Opportunist solves these problems by developing into a Diplomat where their personal needs are subordinated to the social norms. This works well for a time, but eventually the Diplomat is faced with unsolvable problems of needing to follow conflicting social norms. The Diplomat resolves this by transforming into an Expert and finding a craft logic that rules over the social norms. The logic might be based in an ideal of efficiency or it might be based in an ideal of fairness or something else, but it provides a way to resolve the issue of conflicting social pressures. Of course, these logics can conflict and eventually the Expert resolves these conflicts by transforming into the Achiever that shifts between craft logics based on an over-riding goal of organizational effectiveness. Every one of these transitions can be personally traumatic as the very essence of who you are gets turned upside down and changed into something else.

In the terms of this book, the problem for all four stages of conventional development is that they are based in knowing rather than in being curious. They all have a certainty about how the world works and what is important that is almost unquestionable. To make the shift from knowing to being curious requires postconventional development to the Redefining stage and beyond (Table 7.1). For Warren Buffett, this shift

---

[13] This insight come from the work of Bill Torbert and Mary Stacey (2009).

Table 7.1 Action-logics[1]

Opportunistic	Short time horizon, flouts power and sexuality, rejects feedback, hostile humor, deceptive, manipulative, externalizes blame, punishes, views luck as central, punishment rules, views rules as loss of freedom, *eye for an eye* ethic.
Diplomatic	Observes rules, avoids inner and outer conflicts, conforms, suppresses own desires, loyalty to group, seeks membership, right versus wrong attitude, appearance and status conscious, tends toward clichés, works to group standard.
Expert	Interested in problem solving via data, critical of others and self, chooses efficiency over effectiveness, perfectionist, values decisions based on merit, wants own performance to stand out, aware of alternative constructions in problem resolution but can be dogmatic, accepts feedback only from *objective* craft masters.
Achiever	Results and effectiveness oriented, long-term goals, concerned with issues of ethics and justice, deliberately prioritizes work tasks, future inspires, drawn to learning, seeks mutuality in relations, aware of personal patterns of behavior, feels guilty if does not meet own standards, blind to own shadow, chases time.
Shift from knowing to being curious	
Redefining	Collaborative, tolerant of individual difference, aware of context and contingency, may challenge group norms, aware of owning a perspective, inquiring and open to feedback, seeks independent, creative work, attracted by difference and change, may become something of a maverick, focuses on present and historical context.
Transforming	Process and goal oriented, strategic time horizons, systems conscious, enjoys a variety of roles, recognizes importance of principle and judgment, engaged in complex interweave of relationships, aware of own personal traits and shadow, high value on individuality, growth, self-fulfillment, unique market niches, particular historical moments.
Alchemical	Alert to the theatre of action, embraces common humanity, disturbs paradigms of thought and action, dispels notions of heroic action, deeply internalized sense of self-knowledge held with empty mind, sees light and dark, order and mess, treats time and events as symbolic, analogical, metaphorical (not merely linear, digital, literal).

[1] Adopted from the Action Inquiry Associates *Global Leadership Development Profile* created by Bill Torbert and Elaine Herdman-Barker in 2012.

happened in his early 40s when he left the Buffett Partnership and following the advice of his wife Susie, explored a calmer lifestyle. This Redefining stage of development seeks balance between different systems and is usually characterized by a sense of relativism. Of course relativism can be absolutely paralyzing and by his mid-40s, Buffett had developed into the Transforming action-logic with the founding of Berkshire Hathaway. In the Transforming stage, a few most-valued principles rule and provide a way out of the dilemma of relativism. Finally in his early 70s, Buffett develops again to the Alchemical stage as he broadens his focus from just Berkshire Hathaway to the wider world. There are of course, stages beyond the Alchemical, but they are rare in modern society and also very difficult to describe in simple terms. These are the advanced stages of Zen masters and other gurus who are all somewhat incomprehensible to the rest of us. In fact, the few people we encounter who are operating from the Alchemical action-logic usually seem to be rather odd ducks.

I am guessing that by now you are starting to wonder about your own developmental action-logic. I'll take up the question of how you might go about consciously addressing that in the next section, but as a teaser you might ask yourself, which Warren Buffett resonates with your own sense of who you are? Are you most like the awkward college student who reads *How to Win Friends and Influence People*? Or are you driven by a craft logic such as twenty-something Buffett and Graham's value investment approach? Or are you the achievement oriented Buffett of his Buffett Partnership days? You might ask this in terms of who you feel like you are right now, who you are on your best days, and who you are in your worst moments. You might also ask who you want to be as a leader. The research[14] shows that developmental stage is a good predictor of success in leading significant change efforts in organizations and only postconventional leaders have consistent levels of success in doing so. That is not to say that acting from a Transforming orientation guarantees you success as a leader—there are far too many other variables in play and far too many other things that influence how we behave. However, having greater capacity for making sense of the world in more complex ways and being able to be genuinely curious about our own ways of making sense of the world is an enormous advantage for leaders.

It is important to note the difference here between developing more skill or even more skills and developing greater capacity. You could work to become more and more skilled within your current action-logic and

---

[14] Which is conducted by Torbert and associates (Rooke and Torbert 2005; Torbert and Associates 2004).

probably have reasonable amount of success in doing that. It would be analogous to a carpenter becoming better and better at hammering nails. Increasing capacity adds space to your toolbox, it allows you to also have screws, bolts, and complex joinery tools rather than just having a hammer and nails. Of course, you need to work on each of these new skills as you add them to your toolbox, but the point here is that development creates the space for developing a larger repertoire of ways to interact with others. Having more capacity also creates space for being curious. If you only have a hammer, then there is very little point in being curious about whether a screw or bolt or dove-tail joint would be the best way to join two things together—you're going to use your hammer. The same is true for interacting with others. When you develop postconventional ability to be aware of your own frames—to see not only the picture, but also how your frame is determining what you see and don't see—you have options. And given the complexity of human interaction, options are good.

This idea of a developmental journey also answers the question of why it is so difficult to be curious about our own ways of constructing the world, why it is so difficult (and rare) to encounter people who can be open to their interactions with other people in the same way that artists are open to their art. You can learn to stay with your senses and not know, but you also need the cognitive, emotional, and behavioral capacity to not have your sense of self be based in your defining action-logic. To move from knowing to being curious—or from Model I to Model II, or mystery—mastery to collaborative inquiry, or the battle of messages to learning conversations—requires a postconventional level of development. And to make it even harder, we all live in a world that is defined by conventional levels of development. Regardless of the great sages (from Jesus to the Buddha and so many more) that have tried to move us to a collectively more advanced way of seeing the world, it hasn't happened. At least not yet on anything resembling a large scale. All of which is not to say that it's not possible—simply that it is difficult. But many of the worthwhile things in life are difficult. And just maybe, if enough of us try and enough of us succeed, we can get over the hump, past the tipping point and create that elusive postconventional world (in which we all act lovingly toward everyone else and give up attachment and so on). It seems worth a try to me.

Developing Yourself

There are a couple of lessons that we can draw from the idea of the developmental journey. The first is that we are always growing and we can always improve. Reportedly, the legendary cellist, Pablo Casals was once asked why he continued to practice well into his 90s. "Because I think I'm making progress," he answered. All craft masters know there is always progress to be made. This is especially true when it comes to something as complex as interacting with other humans. Another lesson is that our greatest strengths at one point in our journey often become our weakness at the next stage of our journey. The solution to today's problems becomes the source of tomorrow's problems. The craft logic that the Expert adapts in order to solve the problems of being a Diplomat become the source of the problem that must be overcome to grow into an Achiever. The brightest light makes the darkest shadow. Understanding how this plays out in your own story is both important and humbling, but more on that in the next chapter.

There are a variety of ways you can use developmental theory in your own leadership journey. The simplest is to just embrace the ideas in a general way and recognize that you are always growing. You might consciously think about how the ways in which you understand the world are problematic—what are the strengths and weaknesses of your own action-logic? That's easier said than done because for conventional stages of development there is a strong tendency to accept our own action-logic as a basic truth. The sun rises in the east and your action-logic dictates the rules for how things should be done. It is not until we are faced with a painful crisis that we are able to question the action-logic and move beyond it (and not always then). Simply having the idea of a developmental journey in your hip pocket could make you understand those existential crises in a different way—as a chance to grow rather than your whole identity collapsing in upon itself. A deeper understanding (which you would gain from studying it in more depth than simply reading this chapter's brief summary) could also give you some guidance about what the next action-logic looks like and some sense of where you are going on your developmental journey. Part of that deeper understanding is making an estimate of your current developmental level.

When you read the brief descriptions of the action-logics, which one felt the most right to you? Which one felt the most comfortable? Which one felt like what you most aspire to when you are at your best? Which one felt like you when you are at your worst? The answer is probably not the same for each of these questions. We tend to have a *center-of-gravity*[15] action-logic that feels the most comfortable or right to us. But we also tend to have a *fallback* action-logic that we revert to when stressed and we may be aware of an *emergent* action logic that we are aspiring to, but often fail to enact. For example, an engineer might find that her center-of-gravity action logic is Expertise oriented, but when push comes to shove in stressful meetings she falls back into acting from a Diplomatic orientation as she works very hard not to make anyone angry with her—even though she knows that this gets her into trouble and conflicts with her engineering craft logic based in efficiency and effectiveness. She also knows that she has been encouraged to adopt a more achievement-oriented perspective in those very meetings in order to show her manager that she is ready to be promoted to project manager. Thus all three action-logics are in play for her and she can understand this in terms of where she has been, where she is, and where she is going in her developmental journey.

Of course, self-assessments are plagued by our own blindness to our own frames and habitual problematic behaviors. Just as your inquiry group helped you see how you were constructing reality when you did the Learning Pathways Grid or trusted others offered insights into possible improvement goals for the Change Immunity Map, you can also gain a great deal of insight into your action-logics by asking people who know you well how they see you. By now you may well be used to asking for such feedback and the conversation that it leads to will feel like just another learning conversation (which can be difficult to have, but are very useful and enlightening). In addition to the first person self-assessment and the second person assessment from trusted others, there are also validated third person methods for assessing developmental level. These include sentence completion tests such as Action Inquiry Associates Global Leadership Profile (GLP) and the subject—object interview offered

---

[15] The idea of *center-of-gravity fallback*, and *emergent* action-logics comes from the consulting work of Bill Torbert and Elaine Herdman-Barker.

by Bob Kegan and his associates. All of these third person methods require extensive training and should be administered by a qualified professional.

Knowing where you are in your developmental journey provides potential insight into what issues your current frames are solving for you and what problems they may be causing you. It offers a generic view of how you are a genius in both a productive and problematic way. This can be very useful for identifying problematic actual frames and big assumptions and connecting those problematic frames to the bigger picture of your life. It can also be useful for developing plans for how you might frame the world differently to resolve your problems. If your diplomatic orientation is causing you problems, you should try some experiments to enact expertise-oriented frames for the same situation.

You might think of developmental theory as offering a way to go from a blank canvas to an outline of your leadership journey. The stages offer you some guidance, but there is still all of the color and detail of your life to be filled in. There is a great deal of individual variation within each stage and your own personal history and the context of your life matters. You are the genius you are in response to the life you have lived and the times and places in which you have lived. Those early craft masters (many of whom were probably not really masters in any sense of the word), from whom you learned how to interact with other humans—whether that was your parents, a dodgy uncle, a wise aunt, your best friend or mortal enemy who lived next door—matter a great deal. To become a real craft master, you need to understand the details of your own journey.

CHAPTER 8

Becoming the Leader You Want to Be

If the medium of leadership is the interaction between humans, then the tool we have to work on that medium is ourself. The percussionist has her drums, the carpenter, her toolbox of hammers, chisels, saws, and so on, and the leader has herself. The craft master knows her tools. The master leader knows herself. To know yourself is to know your own frames, your big assumptions, your behavioral footprints. But it is also to know your own story—to know why you have those frames and where your big assumptions came from. When you know your own story you not only know your tool, more importantly you have the foundation for making it the story you choose. As the old theater improv adage goes, "if you find yourself in a story you don't like—change it!"[1] By now this should come as no surprise, but just because you have lived your life doesn't mean you know your own story. It takes some work to mine your past to figure out why you are the leader you are right now and who you want to be as a leader going forward.

When you start to look at your own story, it is very common to realize that your parents have had a tremendous impact on who you are as a leader. Often this is a positive impact. But often it is not. Far too often, we discover that we act just like the one person in our life we least wanted to act like. This goes deeper than getting out of bed one morning and hearing yourself make your father's noise when your knees and back hurt. It can be shocking to discover. One of my students tells the following story which came from an inquiry into how she has been interacting with a co-worker.

---

[1] I associate this adage with Nick Nissley who used it to start his TEDx talk in Calgary on narrative leadership in 2010.

Over the past three or four months my co-worker's attitude has changed completely. At one time she was positive and highly productive, and seemed to have a great outlook. Now she complains daily about every little thing that goes wrong. It seems that her challenge is not technical but personal. She is an excellent manufacturing engineer who cares deeply about her responsibilities, but she is having trouble with people who disagree with her.

On numerous occasions, I overhear her complaining about conversations with a multitude of people, from operations supervisors, programmers, hourly employees, and our own manager. I have even been present for some of those conversations, and at times it appears to me that she overreacts and gets emotional when it is unnecessary. If someone teases her in an innocent and joking fashion, she gets upset. If someone disagrees with her on how something is done, she gets upset. Anytime there is conflict in her communications, she gets very emotional.

My initial assessment of the situation is that she needs to "woman up." "Stop whining, stop crying, suck it up, grow up, you're acting like a princess." Other engineers in the group share similar sentiments. We are getting tired of hearing her complain, or even cry in the office. At one point, she even told us how she told our manager how upset she is, how stressful work is, and how hard it is to have school after work and manage having a boyfriend with all her work induced stress. One engineer even replied to her, "how is that our manager's problem?" which brought her to tears.

I began to lose respect for her. Why is she so special? Why is she acting like a princess? Why should others cater to her and treat her differently just because she can't manage her emotions or her time? She needs to "woman up!" I realized that I quickly get angry and judgmental and I fail to see things from her perspective.

Through self-examination I realized that I have become an angry and judgmental person, much like my father. It has reached a point where I look down on others and judge them for not being like I am. Before learning their whole story I assume that they are lazy and full of excuses. It isn't their fault that I had a hard childhood and a poor relationship with my father, or that I was forced to be more mature than most people my age.

Just to give some background on my relationship with my father, I will give some examples of things that put strain on my relationship with him. He does not value women, has no respect for them. They are only meant to cook, clean, and have kids. He did not pay for my college but paid for my brother because he is a male. If he invites us over for dinner I am expected to wash dishes and cook, but my brother isn't. Even in our 20s. He would laugh and judge me when I was emotional, needed guidance. He would resort to physical violence, smashing plates, chairs, punching walls, slapping us in the face, pushing my mom around. He was abused as a child and treated badly. He would always bring it up, but somehow he never connected that he does the same thing to his own family. Because of these things I had no REAL communication or connection with him.

It is frustrating that I have the same urges as he does, but I have felt the effects and would not wish to make others feel the way he made me feel as a child. It is almost as if the anger I feel towards him is similar to the anger I feel towards her when I hear her say childish and selfish things

I remember how emotional I got when trying to reason with my father, and how the more it upset me and the more I fought back, the worse it got. I remember all the emotions of feeling let down, disgraced, extremely angry, alone, judged. Most of all, I remember the feeling that no matter what way I expressed myself he never understood me, and maybe he still doesn't. I'm angry that a person who has such a profound influence on my life was him. I can easily relive those emotions and I have vivid memories of how I felt back then. When I needed him he let me down and made me miserable. I wonder if that is how my co-worker feels right now.

When I take a step back, I realize that this must be the way my co-worker feels when trying to relate to others. She probably feels like we are speaking different languages. I know that is exactly how I felt with my father; it was like we were never on the same page because we had a language barrier.

It sucks that when I hear her say immature, selfish, or childish comments I feel myself becoming him. While I don't agree with what she says, she doesn't deserve someone berating her or putting her down. I wish that my first instinct wasn't to turn into him and let her have it, tell her to woman up, suck it up, nobody cares, you're not a princess so stop acting like one. She is vulnerable and shares with others, and that would only make her feel worse, or make her not want to share her feelings with others. It's so hard for me to be constructive and supportive when it comes to her, but it is worth trying to help.

To be slightly more analytic about this story, she has learned how she tends to deal with difficult emotions (from herself and others) by following the example of how her father dealt with difficult emotions. The answer was to judge the other harshly and blame them for making her feel badly. She knows that she didn't like this strategy when her father used it—she saw him as a hypocrite and it prevented her from feeling a real connection to him. She doesn't want to have this strategy with others; however, it is her natural reaction. In short, she knows what about her own behavior is problematic, and where she learned to behave that way. That provides fertile ground for working on her own craft of leadership. It won't be easy because changing the habits of a lifetime never is and when those are hidden habits of the mind it is all the more difficult. The lesson for all of us here is that most of us have learned how to behave from the important others in our lives when we were young. Those people are usually our parents, but not always. And even though we learn many good and useful ways of behaving, we also often learn to enact the very behaviors that we liked the least in those important others. Most of us, in important ways become our parents.

Not everyone becomes the person (often their father) that they most didn't want to be. Many of us react in the opposite way and become who we are in response to a strong parent. For example, another of my students told this story about why he was so conflict avoidant.

I am afraid to make mistakes, look foolish, or come off as being rude (the way some people "inquire" can be offensive). I will not speak my mind if I think others will not agree or if it will show me as incompetent. Avoiding conflict has shaped my entire existence. As a result, I have become a "chameleon"—able to adapt to the current situation. I behave how I think the person or group I am with will "approve of," and not necessarily what I believe. I have become adept at pushing my own happiness out for the sake of "keeping the peace."

My fears and anxiety around making mistakes and being humiliated have long plagued my actions. I have lived by the famous Abe Lincoln quote "Better to remain silent and be thought a fool than to speak out and remove all doubt."

I grew up in a small town where my father was chief of police. He was the head of the house and he ruled like he ran his department—with an iron fist. Mistakes were not acceptable or tolerated—and God forbid you show ANY emotion. Step out of line—you get the wooden spoon to the back side. Talk back, your mouth gets washed out with soap. My father's favorite expression, which he used often, was: "Children should be seen and not heard—and usually not even seen."

My father taught me that leaders were ruthless dictators and unforgiving disciplinarians who did not accept failure or mistakes of any kind. Winning and succeeding gained positive attention, nothing else mattered. Best to keep your nose clean and mind your own business. This was my way of life for many years.

When I was a teenager, I was sitting in my basement watching a Patriots football game. My dad came down and sat next to me and said we needed to talk. He proceeded to tell me that he and my mom were getting divorced and he was moving out of the house. I couldn't say a word. He got up, made a phone call, and left. I am not sure how long I sat in the cold, dank, musty basement, but it was dark by the time I came upstairs. My mother was nowhere to be found—she never came home that night. Eventually she came home the next day, but she was an absolute emotional wreck—she barely came out of her bedroom and I could hear her constantly crying. To say the family was crushed would be an understatement.

From that moment, my definition of leadership expanded to include adjectives such as self-centered, egotistical, and having the ability to destroy lives. Since I experienced the devastation first hand, I realized I did not want any part of that type of power. I made a decision at that time to avoid having that much control over other people. Leadership has too much responsibility over other people's lives for me to handle. Mistakes by leaders are magnified and the ramifications severe. I didn't even want children, as I did not want to put them through something like this....

This has taken my career and personal life along a path of safety—take very few (well calculated) risks only, don't stick your neck out or cause attention, follow the rules, don't make mistakes at work or in home life.

This is in many ways a classic example of how we develop our frames at an early age. Based upon a few important instances, we create a general theory. His father's behavior did not create a theory of one way that leadership could be, it created a theory of the way that leadership was—and he wanted nothing to do with it. Of course, as an adult, he could see that there are many different ways to be a leader and that he could choose to enact leadership in a way that was congruent with his own values. In his own words:

I finally identified those values I believed made a good leader— generous, empathetic, helpful, and encouraging. A coach, a teacher, a positive role model—those were the kinds of leaders I could admire. It was possible to be a 'good person' and a leader at the same time. Someone that has a desire to make others the best they can be.

Armed with the knowledge of his own story, he can enact a new story. His story is one that takes the drivers of his old story—namely the empathy for others, and the pain from his childhood and his parents' divorce and uses that in a positive way to reframe what it means to be a leader. This is an important point when we are trying to enact a new story—it works best when we are not trying to create too much that is new, but instead making a small change to how we understand our own lives. The change here from "leadership is about controlling and hurting others" to "leadership can be about encouraging and helping others" is entirely consistent with his own lived experience. And it makes all the difference in how he chooses to enact his own leadership story going forward.

All too often we are operating from frames that we developed when we were much younger in response to what was happening in our lives. Those frames become subconscious and remain an unexamined and powerful driver of our behavior, particularly in stressful times when we fall back on our most deeply held beliefs. If we can examine those events and how we have made sense of them from the present, we have the advantage of distance in time and space as well as considerably more sophistication in our thinking—our mind has developed and we can choose to make sense of past events in a more useful (and probably more valid) way.

This process is slightly different for everyone. Here is another one of my students' stories and how he recognized how his past had made him the leader he was and how he wanted to change that to be the leader he wanted to be.

I grew up in a small town in Indiana, and today, I'm going to talk about something that is kind of a big deal in the Midwest: Religion. When I was growing up in Auburn, Indiana, the town's population was around 10,000. It was the largest town in more than twenty miles. It was surrounded by farm country, and the last time I looked in the phone book, there were more than 30 churches. I'm not a particularly religious person today, but I grew up in a religious community. Everyone went to church. My family was Methodist, though it never seemed to matter much what church people went to. Church was a given for everyone I knew. My mother took my sister and me every Sunday. We went to Sunday school, sang in the choirs, and played in the Church bands. I had bible study and bible school in nursery school, during summer vacations, in the youth group during middle school and high school, on my neighbors' front porches—across the street, a few houses down, on the corner, in the middle of the next block.

When I was an adolescent, I went to church camps with group prayers and people sitting in circles. We had to pray out loud individually and share our feelings about our personal relationship with Jesus. No one said anything too different from anyone else. No one said they were uncomfortable with it. It made me nervous, though—the sharing—just a little. And then when I was 13, my youth group attended a concert put on by a Christian evangelist musician—Ray LeFever. At that concert, in between songs, Ray told us about his missionary work. I began to feel uncomfortable as Ray told us he had been a missionary in England. The Methodist Church—my church—comes from England, but Ray told us there was no church in England. There were no Christians. I looked around, and my classmates were swaying to the music and soaking it in. The youth leaders seemed to be doing the same. Ray told us he had been a missionary to skinheads and punks with Mohawks. Ray told us that the last remaining remnants of the Church of England practiced—and I am not making this up—witchcraft.

To this day, not one of my friends attending that concert has ever mentioned they thought anything was strange about it. None of the adults who took us to the event ever said a word—I was left with only tacit approval all around me. And pressure. Ray asked people to put their hands up. He asked us to show how we loved Jesus, and all I could think was how my skin was crawling. I didn't understand what was going on—this guy on the stage was telling us things we all knew were wrong, and all around me, one by one, no one looking at each other—my friends put their hands up. They were swaying to the music. Some of them were crying. Do you know what I did? A 13 year old kid, terribly uncomfortable—I could literally feel the pressure from my peers waiting to see what I would do—willing me to join in. Why was I different? What was wrong with me? I raised my hands, and when Ray asked us all to *promise to live our lives for Christ and give in to the calling of the moment, I promised like everyone else.*

I never liked church again after that, and have come to realize that I blamed myself for not walking out—for not doing something—anything to question what that one second-rate musician was telling us. It is important to me as a mark of character and of leadership to stand up for what you believe in. But it isn't easy, and I couldn't do it. Of course, I also blamed the youth leaders. I realized as I worked through this project that I still blame them to this day—not for the concert, not for Ray—he wasn't important—but for failing us. I thought they were responsible for protecting us and teaching us. I thought they owed us the truth, clarification, acknowledgement of our misunderstandings, and concerns and discomfort. I thought they should show us how to be strong in the face of pressure, but they were part of it. I saw every group prayer differently after that. I quit sharing—I shut down. I felt like I didn't fit, and that I would be judged if I even tried to let anyone know. Those youth leaders probably don't even know the impact they had on me: their inaction—their lack of attention. I believed that they missed an important moment and failed at what I see as the central core of leadership.

Of course I see the whole event a bit differently now. A lot of time has passed. I realize the youth leaders were just volunteer parents trying to keep some adolescents occupied in a positive way. That isn't easy to do in the middle of farm country—options are limited. I think this now, because I have seen myself act the same way. I'm a busy person and don't always think of the people who matter. I get preoccupied with my world and miss what is going on in the world. My wife is fond of telling me any time we get in an argument that I never listen to her. The statement always gets under my skin, especially in those heated moments when I could quote back word for word everything she has said. "It isn't true that I never listen," I always say. "I'm listening right now!" But I know that this isn't the kind of listening she means.

I do the same thing from time to time with co-workers. I once had an intern working for me. The poor kid was woefully unprepared for work as a software developer. He made a website in high school and thought he wanted to cut code for a living. I knew the kid was in over his head, but the company was in financial trouble and everyone was overworked, including me. I tried to break things down in bites he could handle, but I didn't take the time to mentor him *properly, and that was my responsibility. One of our coworkers was constantly badgering him because he was slow to grasp important concepts. I was deep in my own problems, and instead of seeing a drowning intern and having a heart-to-heart with him about whether he really wanted this career, I got annoyed because he took a short assignment from me and did the one thing I told him I wouldn't accept. I told him he had to start over and do the job right, and then I didn't talk to him again. I didn't take the time to listen to what this intern was really saying. A few days later, he started calling in sick and never came back to work again. I don't think it was entirely my fault—he really wasn't cut out for the job. But I could have helped him. I could have helped him see what was obvious to me already, and I could have encouraged him. I could have helped him feel ok about the decision I knew he had to make. But, I didn't. I wasn't trying to be mean; I was just wrapped up in my own problems and didn't pay attention to what my words and my inaction were telling that kid.*

You can miss the suffering on someone's face. You can overlook their body language. You can hear every word someone says and not listen to them at all. You can understand each syllable, the phrases, the sentences and how they all fit together, but miss the meaning completely. I know because I do it all too often. I share my opinion or answer questions confidently and too quickly—sometimes before I hear the last word; sometimes before I hear the real question after the last word or lurking somewhere between the lines. I answer and move on before I catch that the real problem has nothing to do with any of the words. Sometimes I know I am not really trying; my wife is right, I don't always listen, and listening—really listening in a profound way—is what leaders have to do. Leadership is not just about what you say. It isn't even mainly about what you say. It is about what you do and how you treat other people. It's about doing what it takes to help those people to whom you are responsible find their way. Leadership is about service to others, and serving others means listening—not just sometimes, but all the time.

This is what I wish my church youth leaders had done for us during that concert years ago. I wish someone had seen me and said something. Just a nod and a laugh—just a phrase: "Yeah this experience is getting a little intense, isn't it?" and a smile, and the lonely discomfort and pressure would have lost some power. This attentiveness is what I hope to have the strength to provide others. This is the type of leader I want to be.

Again, we see the same basic ingredients—an event (or events) from the past, usually traumatic in some way (those seem to stick with us more than the happy ones) that has deeply informed how we see the world. There is an implication of how those early frames are problematic in the here-and-now. And finally, a reframing that is consistent with the experienced events, but takes them in a different and more positive direction. Here, the event is not being listened to, nor being protected by the youth leaders. This led to him mirroring that behavior in his own life and learning to not listen to others and staying wrapped up in his own world. The reframing is that the better response—the response he wants to have to be the leader he wants to be (and wishes others were when he was young)—is to listen, really listen beyond the words, to the actions of others.

This sort of self-understanding, knowing your own story and the story you want to enact is the foundation for developing your own leadership craft. It tells you where the edge of your own practice is, what you are trying to do, what is difficult (but really important) for you to do, and even in what contexts that is likely to be most difficult. Working on that edge of practice is where we get better at being a leader, it's where our skills develop and we engage with the developmental transformations discussed in the last chapter. The edge of our practice changes over time and most of us have several different edges of our own practice that we can work on at any given time. But, the true craft master is always working on the edges of their own practice.

Even though you have lived your life, you probably don't know your life story. Or perhaps more accurately, you know one (or maybe even a couple) version of your life story, which probably isn't the one you need to know. I have had countless students tell me that there haven't been any big events in their life, certainly nothing worth talking about, and they couldn't possibly tell the sort of story that I quoted in the last section. Of course, they are all wrong, and they all find plenty of things to talk about. But not without some help—from the insight of others (usually their inquiry group members) and from doing a couple of exercises. We don't know our life story because we lived it. What was normal and unexceptional to us, may well be interesting and obviously important in developing who we are to others. So the way to learn your life story is to tell it to others (and yourself). There are many stories you can tell—everyone's life can be told in countless different ways, including some events and not including others. I use two exercises to help you learn your own story—six-word autobiographies and the river of life.

Six-Word Autobiographies

Six-word autobiographies are exactly what they sound like—your life story in six words.[2] It is, of course, impossible to tell your whole life story in six words. But, it is possible to tell a version of your life story in six words. You can write as many six-word autobiographies as you would like. Smith Magazine has a website[3] devoted to six-word autobiographies, which includes the following celebrity offerings:

"The miserable childhood leads to royalties"

– Frank McCourt

"German-Jews. Dyslexia. Acting. Family. Writing. Complete."

– Henry Winkler

"I'm so tired, I'm awake again."

– Chelsea Handler

And one of my favorites from one of my students is:

"Trying not to be an asshole."

Distilling your life down to six words requires that you find a common thread of meaning in your life. Because it is only six words, you know that you have to leave almost everything out so you don't need to feel guilty about getting it wrong. You will get it wrong in most ways, but you may also get it right in some important way. And it can be fun—you can do it as part of your dinner conversation if you'd like. It doesn't take

---

[2] This exercise was inspired by the book, *Not quite what I was planning: Six-word memoirs by writers famous and obscure* (Fershleiser and Smith 2008).

[3] It's http://sixwordmemoirs.com/about/celebrity-six-world-memoirs/

very long, so you can do it several times. It may feel rather odd at first—if you've never told the story of your life, telling it in six words can be a daunting task. Nonetheless, it is a good way to start the process of understanding your own leadership story.

The River of Life

Where the six-word autobiography asked you to tell your life story very succinctly, the river of life offers more room by asking you to draw your life story using the visual metaphor of a river. The exercise is usually facilitated, but you can do it on your own.[4] The basic idea is to imagine your life as a river, with the start of the river being when you were born. The river then flows along and different aspects of the river represent different events and phases of your life. There may be places where the river splits in two—forming an island. There may be rapids or waterfalls that show particularly turbulent times in your life. You may choose to include creeks and other tributaries that represent something that had a big influence on your life. You can use whatever sorts of imagery that feel right to you—that could include people having a picnic on the banks of the river or sharks swimming in the eddies or something else entirely. The river may run straight or it may twist and turn—perhaps each turn is a developmental transformation? It is your life; it can look however you want it to look.

When I facilitate a group in the process of drawing the river of life, I start with a brief guided meditation. I ask them to imagine being in a hot air balloon and drifting along over the river that is their life, moving from the present, back to when they were born. I then ask them to draw what they saw. After a suitable time to draw I ask them to imagine they are back in the same hot air balloon, only this time they turn on a speaker and they can hear sounds from the river. This time as they float down the river,

---

[4] The book, *Leadership Presence* (Halpern and Lubar 2003) includes a nice version of the river of life in an appendix. My own version is based on that as well as various skilled facilitators' versions that I have been lucky enough to experience at different times in my life.

they hear the sounds of their life. I then give them more time to work on their drawing, including what they heard. Again, after a suitable time I ask them to imagine they are back in the hot air balloon again. This time, I tell them that balloon is floating very near the surface of the river and I ask them to notice the smells of their life as they drift along. I then give them a final bit of time to add what they have smelled to their drawing.

The river of life drawings that are produced, vary a great deal, which you can see in the four examples in Figures 8.1 through 8.4. They can be simple or complex, contain no text or a lot of text, be aesthetically lovely or somewhat childish. It doesn't matter. What matters is what you do with your river of life. Here again, others' insights are critical, so once you have drawn your river of life, you need to use it to tell the story of your life to others. Your audience can then feedback to you what they have heard—what are the interesting parts, which events seem to have been really important, and what themes they hear that cross different parts of your life. Their perspective will give you useful perspective on your own story.

You could simply tell others your life story without doing these exercises. You could write your autobiography.[5] However, there is something powerful in the transmodal aspect of both the six-word autobiography and the river of life. By transmodal, I mean that the exercises ask you to shift between different modes of representing your story. The six-word biography asks you to use language in a very concise and poetic way. The river of life asks you to shift from words to images. These shifts in modes of representation often give us a new way of understanding the subject. Just as giving a presentation on it can change how we understand a report that we have written, the shift between different modes gives us a new perspective—and getting different perspectives on our own life is both difficult (because we have lived it from our own singular perspective) and useful (so that we can reframe and move forward enacting the story we choose to live).

---

[5] I have found that the *Felt Sense* (Perl 2004) approach to writing is very useful for this sort of work.

Figure 8.1 A River of life

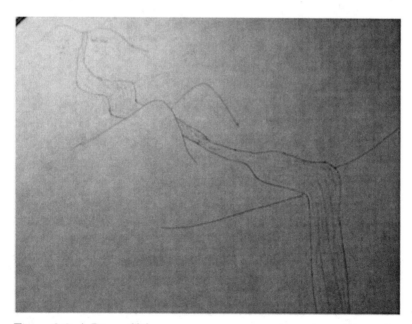

Figure 8.2 A River of life

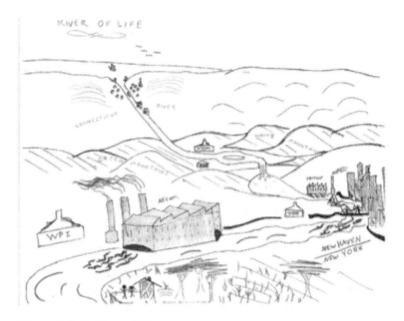

Figure 8.3 A River of life

Figure 8.4 A River of life

Leading from Your Story

The stories presented in the first part of this chapter are from an exercise that I ask my students to do—to tell the story of who they are as a leader and who they want to be as a leader. It is something that you do in a class, not something that you would do in your day-to-day practice as a leader. However, even though you may never tell that story in your day-to-day life, it is worth knowing that story and worth practicing telling it. Knowing the story tells you where to dig for leadership gold and telling the story creates connection with others. Let's look at each of those in turn.

When I say knowing the story tells you where to dig, it means that your leadership story tells you where the edge of your practice is. You might think of your leadership journey as a treasure hunt in which you are looking for mastery of the craft of leadership. In any treasure hunt, you need two things: you need to know where to dig and you need to know how to dig. The tools such as the Ladder of Inference, Learning Pathways Grid, and Change Immunity Map are all tools for digging. But it doesn't do a lot of good to know how to dig if you don't know where to dig. You need a treasure map. And your own leadership story is the treasure map that tells you where to dig.

Telling your story, or perhaps more accurately telling parts of your stories, is a powerful tool for creating connection with others. If leadership happens in the interactions with other people, then the medium of leadership is connection between people. As a leader you want to create and strengthen those connections so you have more to work with. There are many ways to create connections between people and not all of them are positive. You can create powerful connections based in dependency or fear. But you can also create powerful connections based in mutual respect, trust, and even love. It's your choice as a leader, but I am going to focus on creating those more positive connections and how telling parts of your stories helps to do that.

At one end of the scale of the sort of connection we can create with others is love. Why do we love someone? Let's focus on the type of love we have for friends and family rather than romantic love and all that involves. I don't claim to have any sort of definitive understanding, but it seems to me that there is usually a mix of having things in common, respect, and shared experiences. There's no substitute for having grown up together and spent countless hours together—you know (and love) those lifelong friends in a way that most people you are trying to lead will never know you. But, telling parts of your stories can serve to create some of the same sorts of connection. If you can open you heart and share a part of yourself, others can start to feel like they know you a bit. If you can tell the right story, it can serve to not only start to create that sort of connection, but it can also normalize self-stigmatized, problematic behaviors and show the way forward (and isn't that what leadership often is—showing the way forward?).

As an example of what I mean, imagine the last storyteller (the one about religion and really listening) telling a portion of that story to one of his direct reports who had trouble listening to others. He could talk about his own troubles in that area and why he had a tendency to retreat into his own shell and not listen to others. When done well, this serves to normalize the behavior—lots of people do this (it's not just you, it's me, too)—and show that it is possible (but not easy) to work on the issue and get better at it. It creates some common (maybe even somewhat shared) experience that helps create connection. And it may even induce a little respect by showing that he was able to get better at it and often create some connection just by being vulnerable and admitting to some weakness. Again, I have to admit that I am not completely sure what all is going on when you tell authentic leadership stories,[6] but I do know that time and again it works to create deeper and better, positive connections.

Sharing who you are and who you are trying to be as a leader, also makes your commitment to being that sort of leader public and thus discussable. It is an invitation for others to help you in becoming the leader you want to be (but struggle to be). You could also say that is an invitation for others to call you on it when you don't live up to your ideals. In that way it can help keep you humble—nothing keeps me humble like having my own behavioral hypocrisy pointed out to me. Humility and help from others are two things that every craft master needs to continually improve their craft.

---

[6] Although, I have spent considerable time theorizing this and writing about it (Ladkin and Taylor 2010; Taylor 2012, 2013a, 2015).

There are countless tools and techniques for working on the craft of leadership that I have not talked about here—bookstores are filled with volumes dedicated to them. I am sure you will find some of them helpful and others not so much. As someone dedicated to your craft, you should stay curious about and open to new ways to improve your craft— complacency with your own practice is an enemy of craft mastery. I now turn to offering a longer example of what this sort of continual working on becoming the leader you want to be can look like.

CHAPTER 9

Working on Your Craft: An Example

Throughout this book, I have used examples taken from the work of my students (with their permission and sometimes melded together into composites). Hopefully, these examples have been helpful for showing how to use the tools to actively work on the craft of interacting with other people. Here, I'd like to step aside and offer a fuller example of a completed inquiry in the student's own words. The names and other unimportant details have been changed to hide their identities, but the story is all his. This is Jack's story, chronicling how he came to understand more about his practice and his struggles with his own leadership. It spans a couple of months in a university semester, but connects back to a lifetime of practice and hints at what might be involved in becoming a master.

Being a genius of self-protection is not all it's cracked up to be. If we do not confront our subconscious frames and assumptions then we waste an awful lot of energy sabotaging our own commitments. In certain situations, my own simple commitments to being open and honest are subconsciously undermined and my relationships become poisoned with bottled bitterness and resent. Through inquiry and reflective practice I uncover the saboteur and disempower him with the light of day and reason ... and experiments.

Two-Column Case #1: Conversation with Fred

The following conversation occurred last year. My in-laws, Fred and Amy, own and operate a reforestation business in Alajuela, Costa Rica, and we live down there a few months each year. In order to eliminate the need for multiple cellular internet contracts, Fred had been experimenting unsuccessfully for weeks with a wireless bridge between his house and Javier's house. The two properties are separated by half a kilometer of forest. One day I found myself struggling to work because of chainsaw noise. When I followed the noise I discovered that Nicanor, one of Fred's employees, was clearing trees between the two properties.

What I thought and felt	What was said
You have got to be out of your fracking mind. Look at this disaster. Why would Fred do this?	Me: (Yelling over the chainsaw noise, in Spanish) Hello! Nicanor!
	Nicanor: (Turns off chainsaw). Hello, Jack. How are you?
I feel frustrated and angry, but I am not sure how to articulate that in Spanish although I am sure it shows my body language and tone.	Me: Nicanor, why are you felling these trees?
	Nicanor: Because Fred instructed me to.
That confirms my suspicion and makes me feel even angrier at Fred for ordering the destruction of these trees.	Me: This is not good. I thought we were in the business of reforestation. I am going to talk to Fred.

Nicanor resumes cutting down trees, and there is nothing I can do to stop him because I have no authority over him, nor do I have sufficient command over the language to persuade him otherwise. So I march back to the house, angry and disappointed that Fred would sacrifice rainforest to save $20 per month on his stupid internet connection. Back at the house I find Fred lying in front of the television, which is par for the course for him lately.

What I thought and felt	What was said
My heart is pounding, I am starting feel sweaty, and this is not a conversation I want to have.	Me: (Noticeably agitated, but polite) Excuse me, Fred, did you know that Nicanor is cutting down trees behind the house?
	Fred: Oh that. Yea, he is clearing some brush.
Wow, you are such a fracking lair. Those are trees that Nicanor is cutting, not brush. Let me test my hypothesis through some inquiry.	Me: Are you sure? It looks to me like he is cutting down trees so that you can get your wireless bridge working. Is that what is really going on?
	Fred: Well, yes, but those are really just weeds he is cutting down. So I'm really doing the rainforest a favor by having them cut down.
He is lying to me and to himself to justify his actions. Even though I am still angry and frustrated, I feel helpless and afraid to push the conversation further.	Me: Okay.

This interaction, although not problematic perhaps when viewed externally, is hugely problematic internally because I become furious and unable to seek resolution. Steven Taylor writes that "often simply seeing an interaction written down as a two-column case provides enough distance to start to see how our own behavior is contributing to the problematic nature of the situation." What is my behavior? What is the problematic nature? That I become angry and emotional during this conversation is to be expected, feeling emotion is what makes us human. Rather it is my active restraint and reluctance to express myself that contributes to the problematic situation. That inaction acts to pressurize and bottle my anger, only to ferment later into bitterness and resent.

Analysis Using the Ladder of Inference

To analyze this conversation, I return to Steven Taylor "We can use the idea of the Ladder of Inference as an analytic tool to slow down the meaning making process and look at how we moved from the data to how we made meaning and acted upon that meaning."

The actual data that I have is that Fred ordered Nicanor to fell trees. And I name that data to myself as "Fred is cutting down the rainforest." From that I inferred that Fred is a liar who does not care about the rainforest. I made that inference based on my frames that people's actions better represent their priorities than their words.

Data: Fred is cutting down the rainforest.
Inference: Fred is a liar who does not care about the rainforest.
Frame: When someone's actions contradict their words, then they are liars.

This Ladder of Inference is simple and certainly sounds reasonable. But it does not explain my strong emotional reaction or subsequent conflict avoidance. When I think about it, people say one thing and do another thing all the time. Yes, that bothers me, and yes I label them as liars. But that frame generally does not provoke a strong emotional reaction or substantively affect my interactions with these liars. This leads me to believe that there must be some alternative frames and inferences that have greater significance on my thoughts and feelings.

> Data: Fred is cutting down the rainforest to save money (on his internet).
> Inference: Fred is a self-centered, greedy bastard.
> Frame: People who sacrifice the rainforest to save petty cash are self-centered, greedy bastards.

Fred did not cut those trees to feed a starving family or find a cure for cancer. Fred cut them down to save a comparably small amount of money. That data provides context for his actions, and that contextual data provoked an emotional reaction for several reasons. First I believe that people who sacrifice natural resources to save nickels and dimes are greedy bastards and contribute unnecessarily to planetary destruction. Second, Fred's actions contradicted a preexisting and reasonably-founded frame where I assumed he cared deeply about the rainforest. When he contradicted my frame about him, it just added fuel to the fire. So why couldn't I express my emotions or confront him on the issue? That is the essence of this inquiry project.

Two-Column Case #2: Conversation with My Team

Many interactions are through e-mails, instant messenger, voicemail, and other asynchronous channels. This e-mail conversation is about a recent team project in our accounting class. These projects occur weekly and account for 50 percent of our accounting grade. Before leaving on a weekend hiking trip, I wrapped up my contribution to our team document and then communicated my progress along with some additional thoughts. This e-mail conversation is highly paraphrased to remove most nonessential details and identifying information.

What I thought and felt	What was said
Why do I have to make these suggestions? My teammates should be doing this already.	Me: Here is a list of stuff I did, and here are my thoughts.
	Armand: Jack, I had a commitment tonight and will read and edit in the morning.

How condescending! You know, I have commitments and I contribute to our team projects in a timely fashion.	Charles: Here is a list of stuff I did and my thoughts.
There was a break of about 24 hours (Saturday a.m.–Sunday a.m.) where no e-mails occurred.	
	François: Here is a list of stuff I did. Felix and Armand, I will submit the paper after you make changes and sign off.
	Armand: François, I want to watch the Patriots game tonight. Let me know when you are done so I can submit the paper.
Is this another of your so-called commitments?	Felix: François, please review our part. I mentioned some tools. Take them out if you don't think they fit.
Argh! Seriously? You wait until the last fracking minute, you do 10 minutes of work, and you get the same credit as everyone else on this team. This is infuriating!	François: Felix, your changes were great! Just submitted the memo. Thanks for all your hard work!
What the frack! Why do you encourage this behavior? They were not great changes. It was too little, too late. This happens with every single project. Now I am just frosted, but I feel helpless and afraid to share my feelings or confront teammates about their behaviors. I suck it up and try to get over it.	Jack: (says nothing)

The core problem with this asynchronous conversation parallels my live conversation with Fred. Although I am angry and emotional, I actively avoid expressing my feelings and leave those emotions bottled up. Since this conversation was not synchronous, I had more time to react (or not) and feel emotions. That the pattern of behavior repeated itself in an asynchronous conversation though, I feel is significant and worth exploring further.

Analysis Using the Ladder of Inference

There is a lot of data in this e-mail conversation, but the nuance that really provoked the most negative emotion was the late response by Felix, which I name to myself as "Felix barely contributed to our team project." From that I inferred that Felix is a freeloader, and that inference is based on my frame that people who accept credit for work which they did not do are freeloaders. The timing of responses in an asynchronous conversation can correlate with actions, and here the timing of those actions was a key element to this interaction.

> Data: Felix barely contributed to our team project, and only at the last minute.
> Inference: Felix is a freeloader.
> Frame: People who get credit for work they did not do are freeloaders.

That frame may seem a bit extreme in a situation like this, and perhaps I could have applied an alternative and plausible frame that would give Felix the benefit of the doubt. But during the conversation, because of my frames and inferences, I became angry at Felix, and angry at the situation. And just like my earlier conversation with Fred, I thought about saying something, and felt like I should say something, but instead I bottled up my emotion and said nothing which only made things worse in the long run.

Another piece of this asynchronous conversation provoked strong negative emotions too. Toward the end of the e-mail chain, François wrote, "Felix, your changes were great!" From this I draw that François praised Felix for his contribution. My inference is that François is a coward. That inference stems from my frame that people who avoid saying what needs to be said are cowards.

> Data: François praised Felix for his contribution which was last-minute and minimal.
> Inference: François is a coward.
> Frames: People who avoid saying what needs to be said are cowards.

In retrospect, this is an interesting situational frame that I apply to other people precisely because I have never applied it to myself. By not saying anything, by not expressing how the situation made me feel, and by not saying what needed to be said, then by the same logic I too must be a coward! Did you catch that? When I apply my own frame about others, onto myself, it implies that I am coward.

Remarkable though as it may seem, I am not a coward. Actually I am a genius of self-protection. Yes, a genius. By not speaking up with Felix, I prevent myself from having a difficult conversation with Felix about his substandard work. This again is the essence of my inquiry project.

Analysis Using the Learning Pathways Grid

To uncover and understand the frames that I subconsciously applied during this interaction, I now employ the Learning Pathways Grid (LPG). The LPG process allowed me to work backwards from the desired and actual outcomes of the asynchronous interaction, through actions that caused those outcomes, and ultimately to the actual frames that influenced and provoked my actions.

Actual frames	Actual actions	Actual outcomes
People who get credit for work they did not do are freeloaders, and freeloaders are untrustworthy, bad people.	I contribute my fair share Felix slacks off I retreat from any confrontation	Emotional outcomes I felt angry at Felix I felt frustrated with the situation
Fallout from a confrontation gone sour will damage common relationships.		I felt cheated and defrauded I felt afraid to confront Felix
If I confront someone about their behavior, they may perceive it as a personal attack.		I felt helpless Relational outcomes I lost trust in Felix
People who feel they have been personally attacked will distance themselves from me.		I lost respect for Felix I did not cause friction Instrumental outcomes I did not share my feelings I did not confront Felix I bottled my anger

Desired frames	Desired actions	Desired outcomes
Nobody wants to be a freeloader. Nobody wants to be a bad teammate. People want to be told when they are causing problems. Strong relationships are the product of honesty and openness. If I do not confront negative behavior it will fester and harm relationships.	Confront negative behavior before it starts to fester. Withhold judgment and give people the benefit of the doubt until discussing the behavioral problem with them.	Emotional outcomes To feel comfortable confronting teammates when something is bothering me To feel satisfied with team projects To not get angry or frustrated Relational outcomes To trust my teammates To feel valued by my teammates Instrumental outcomes To speak up when I have issues To hold teammates accountable

According to the Scrolls of Pythia in the reimagined Battlestar Galactica television series, "All this has happened before. All this will happen again." This obscure passage about predetermined destiny reflects how I feel whenever we embark on another project, which itself is an interaction. The sequence of actual actions almost becomes predictable: I will contribute, Felix will slack off, and then I will avoid confronting Felix about the situation. This pattern of action has plagued me throughout my adolescent and adult life. It happened in high school, it happened in college, it happened in graduate school, it happened in the workplace, and according to the oracle Pythia, it will happen again.

What frames do I apply that contribute to this recurring sequence of actions?

The first action, that I contribute my fair share (or more) to team projects, stems from my commitments to being a top performer and from being a dependable teammate. By definition, as a top performer I hold myself to high performance expectations. But perhaps ironically (after all, we can't all be top performers), I project my high expectations of myself onto my teammates. This may unintentionally set up team situations for negative outcomes. Why? Because when team performance does not meet my high expectations, it provokes negative emotions such as disappointment, anger, and distrust. Generally speaking, team performance does not meet my high expectations, and in turn provokes negative emotions. However, it happens all the time, and the degree of negativity is ridiculously higher when the full pattern of actions in my LPG occurs.

The second action triggered several negative emotions. When Felix did not contribute to our team project and received academic credit without earning it, I subconsciously applied my frame that people who get credit for work they do not do are freeloaders. Felix was a freeloader and this made me feel cheated, defrauded, and angry because he took my work ethic for granted and essentially got credit for my work. My relationship with Felix suffered too because my trust and respect for him diminished. Retrospectively the frame I applied to this action does not seem irrational, unjust, or unreasonable. However, I hold another frame about freeloaders: nobody wants to be a freeloader. Perhaps had I applied this desired alternative frame, I may not have reacted so negatively to the situation.

The third action was one of avoidance. Although I felt logically justified and emotionally fueled to confront Felix about the situation, the prospect of actually doing so horrified me. My subconscious frames about confrontation triggered a retreat. Through discussion and reflection, I discovered a set of three interrelated protective frames that contributed to this action of avoidance.

- If I confront someone about their behavior, they will perceive it as a personal attack.
- People who feel they have been personally attacked will distance themselves from me.
- Fallout from a confrontation gone sour will damage common relationships.

The fear and avoidance caused by these frames resulted in bitterness, bottled anger, distrust, and continued avoidance. It was a negative feedback loop. Although I tried to keep the emotional elephant caged and hidden away, my bottled emotions leaked into my relationships with Felix and other teammates. The frames that were meant to protect me ended up hurting me.

The three relationship frames uncovered in my LPG analysis were causing problems. On the surface they seemed reasonable. But through reflection, inquiry, and analysis it became clear to me that they invoke fear and avoidance. They are undesired frames and I would like to replace them with these following frames, which together provoke action and resolution:

- Teammates want to be told when they are causing problems.
- Strong relationships are the product of honesty and openness.
- If I do not confront negative behavior, it will fester and harm relationships.

Remarkably though, I am already committed to holding and applying these frames. For instance, openness and honesty are already part of my identity. Yet situations arise where my undesired frames trump my desired frames, and my resulting actions run counter to my commitment to being open and honest. In order to weed out the competing commitments that are driving my behavior and preventing me from being open and honest, I turn to another tool called the Change Immunity Map.

Change Immunity Map

Commitment	Doing/not doing	Competing commitment	Big assumption
Being open and honest	Not communicating my frustration when behavioral issues arise. Avoiding interactions with people with whom I am frustrated and angry. Venting my frustration to my wife, albeit without solving the problem.	Do not want to damage relationships	If I am open and honest about a negative behavior or situation then it might directly damage our relationship or indirectly damage other relationships.

"Strong relationships are the product of honesty and openness" is one of the desired frames that emerged from the LPG analysis. Truly I am committed to being open and honest, even in situations that I perceive as confrontational. How hard could it be? I mean, I am already almost always open and honest. Yet there are certain interactions, like my face to face conversation with Fred, or like my asynchronous interaction with Felix, where I refrain from being open and honest.

In potentially confrontational situations, instead of being open and honest, I do this instead:

- I choose to withhold my feelings, especially when my issues involve personal or behavioral issues. When Fred cut down the trees, I became angry with the situation and with Fred. How dare he contradict my pre-established assumptions about his personal values! When Felix did not contribute to our team project, I became angry with the situation and with Felix. How dare he take advantage of my amazing work ethic!
- I avoid interactions with people with whom I am frustrated and angry. This avoidance causes anger and negative emotions to fester and evolve into bitterness and resent.
- I vent my frustration to my wife. The venting helps because she sympathizes with my situation and makes me feel temporarily better. But venting does not address the underlying issue. So when the unresolved situation reemerges (and it always does), my negative emotions return stronger than ever, and now they are peppered with bitterness and resentment.

So what competing commitment is driving these problematic behaviors? When I imagine confronting Fred with my negative feelings about his behavior (cutting down the rainforest), I feel a fear of retribution. The threat of personal attack does not bother me. But I am scared that Fred would hold a grudge, or that Fred would adversely influence my relationships with my mother-in-law or with other relationships that we share. When I imagine confronting Felix with my negative feelings about his behavior (poor team contributions), I feel a similar fear of retribution. The confrontation could cause Felix to distance himself from me. Or he might negatively influence my relationships with other MBA cohorts. It seems that my competing commitment is a drive to preserve my relationships. For some reason I feel like my direct and shared relationships would become threatened were I to confront someone about their behavior.

What experience in my life caused me to learn this pattern of behavior? Why do I think that confronting people about behavioral issues will damage relationships? The answer is neither comfortable to write about nor comfortable to accept. But here it is. When I was three years old, my parents divorced. It was an ugly divorce. Their heated arguments reverberated through the house. The ensuing custody battle and separation ripped apart my family and its effects rippled through my childhood. Family friends became friends of Charles or friends of Laura, never both. Legally I was only allowed to visit my father two days every two weeks and much of that was spent in the car. The fallout from their divorce affected my relationships with my mother and father. It taught me that direct conflict will directly and adversely affect a relationship and it will have indirect fallout that affects other relationships (like mine). Is it any wonder I have avoided personal conflict all my life?

This big assumption of course is that if I am open an honest about a negative behavior or situation then the other person might directly damage our relationship and indirectly damage other relationships too. It sounds plausible in certain situations perhaps. But rationally it does not make much sense in the context of my two-column case interactions. Rationally, I should expect that confronting people openly and honestly when their behavior bothers me will result in a positive outcome. And that is a testable hypothesis.

Planning Experiments: My Hypothesis

Context	Old frames	Old actions	Old outcomes
When I have an issue with someone else's behavior and When that person is someone I must continue working with or someone I care about and When I share other relationships with that person which could be influenced by that person	Fallout from a confrontation gone sour will damage common relationships. If I confront someone about their behavior, they may perceive it as a personal attack. People who feel they have been personally attacked will distance themselves from me.	I withhold my feelings, especially when my issues involve personal or behavioral issues I avoid interactions with people with whom I am frustrated and angry	I continue holding negative emotions about the situation. I become bitter and resentful toward that person. I may do extra work to compensate for the poor behavior I may become demotivated to work with that person again

Planning Experiments: My Planned Approach

Context	New frames	New actions	New outcomes
When I have an issue with someone else's behavior and When that person is someone I must continue working with or someone I care about and When I share other relationships with that person which could be influenced by that person	Strong relationships are the product of honesty and openness. People want to be told when they cause problems. If I do not confront negative behavior it will fester and harm relationships.	Proactively seek out people for discussion when I have issues with their behavior. Be open and honest about my feelings. Trigger: When I feel negative emotion about someone else. Action: Schedule a personal conversation with that person.	I will have stronger relationships. I will not feel bitter and resentful towards others with whom I've had issues. I will demonstrate to others that it is okay to express emotion (i.e., leading by example). I will help build more effective teams (i.e., improve the team dynamic).

Experiment #1: Planning

For my first experiment, I decided to heed my own advice and confront Felix. My primary goals were to overcome my avoidance of the situation and express my feelings openly and honestly. Initiating the interaction was easily accomplished by scheduling a private meeting with Felix over the telephone. But actually being open and honest about my feelings about his behavior was not going to be easy. Even after doing all of this analysis, just thinking about it scared me. To better prepare for the meeting I prepared the following plan of action.

In the early conversation, I aimed to articulate my key points early instead of beating around the bush.

- I feel like you are not contributing to team projects.
- It feels unfair to me because I believe everyone should earn their grade by contributing.
- It is negatively affecting how I feel about working on this team.

Then I brainstormed several possible ways in which Felix might respond. For each of these response scenarios, I preformulated some tactics and specific phrases to progress the conversation toward a more desirable outcome.

Response scenario	Tactics and possible phrases
He may say nothing at all	Inquire: Felix, I really need to hear what you think about this.
He may get defensive. And/or He may completely disagree and become offended. And/or He may go on the attack	Inquire: How much time and effort did you put into the Acuaponicos case? How much time and effort did you put into our marketplace decisions this week? How much time and effort did you put toward the Alltel case three weeks ago? If response is: "small amount of time," then balance advocacy and illustration The projects are 50 percent of our grade. To me, that means we should invest half of our time on these projects, or about six hours per week. On the Alltel case, I spent invested several hours working with François asynchronously on the CVP model, and then several more hours contributing to the written memo. When I do not see you contributing earlier in the week, I try to pick up the slack. But other areas of my life are suffering, and quite frankly it is neither sustainable nor fair. The minimum required effort, as Bill and Karen said in January, is about 12 hours per week per course. Do you feel the contributions you are making reflect that commitment? If response is: "moderate or large amount of time" then be more direct. Your contributions as I perceive them do not reflect what you're telling me. But I do not even feel you are doing C level work. Frankly I would be okay with C level work.
He may completely agree but make a series of excuses	Possible responses, mixture of framing, and advocacy When I applied to the cohort program, I committed to pull my weight. Right now I feel like our team and this program are your last priority. And I need to know whether I can depend on you to pull your weight too. Can you make more substantive contributions earlier in the week? When I do not see you contributing earlier in the week, I try to pick up the slack. But other areas of my life are suffering, and quite frankly it is neither sustainable nor fair. The minimum required effort, as Bill and Karen said in January, is about 12 hours per week per course. Do you feel the contributions you are making reflect that commitment? But I perceive that you are hardly doing anything in comparison to the rest of the team, so we have to contribute extra or take a hit in our team performance. Do you see any other options?
He may completely agree and resolve to change	Felix, I am very glad that you want to fix this. I need to know that I can depend on you to do your portion of the work. Specifically, I need to see you do your work earlier in the week, and I need to see more substantive contributions.

Experiment #1: Execution and Reflection

The actual conversation with Felix was much longer and more detailed than the two column case I present here. For brevity, and to respect Felix's privacy, I withheld some personal details. Here is a paraphrased version that captures the essence of the conversation.

What I thought and felt	What was said
	Jack: Well I am not sure how to say this, so please let me say what I need to say and then we can talk about it together. Felix, I feel you are not contributing much to team projects and it bothers me because everybody receives the same grade on a group project, and I believe that everyone needs to earn that grade by contributing roughly equally. It is its negatively affecting how I feel about working on this team and it is affecting my performance too.
Wow! I feel like a huge weight has been lifted just for expressing my feelings and how this situation affects me.	Felix: I appreciate you saying that and I completely agree with what you are saying. I am really sorry. I have a lot of excuses, but that is beside the point. I will prioritize this program.
Wow again! That debunks my old frames already, plus I feel genuinely better. Ultimately though his actions will show me whether he really means what he says here.	Jack: I am glad to hear you want to fix this. I want to know that I can depend on you to do your portion of the work going forward.
Crap! That sounded too aggressive. Hopefully he did not hear it that way.	Felix: Thanks. I don't want to consume too much of your morning. Let me just say again that I am very sorry and I want to you to know that I am committed to doing my share of the work.
Awesome!	Jack: That's good. Thank you Felix, I appreciate it.

Bravo to me! Today I confronted one of my biggest fears and actually confronted someone to share my feelings about their behavior. And it felt great. This experiment demonstrated that my new desired frames can indeed invoke positive actions, and those positive actions help to achieve my desired outcomes. By confronting Felix I shattered my fermenting, festering bottle of emotions. Felix said outright that he appreciated my openness and honesty, which supports my frame that people want to be told when they are causing problems.

In subsequent interactions, Felix seemed more forthcoming with his ideas, and he communicated his expectations of himself more to the team. He started contributing more and participating more to our team decisions and discussions last week too. My own emotions about this situation have shifted toward the positive end of the spectrum. This experiment demonstrates to me that honesty and openness can really build stronger relationships, and can really build more effective teams. This interaction also disconfirmed some of my assumptions from our prior interactions. Felix was not intentionally taking advantage of the team. He had his reasons. But he meant no harm and cared enough about our relationship and the team dynamic to enact changes.

Experiment #2: Planning, Execution, and Reflection

My second experiment was much less scary because my first experiment was so successful and because I was excited (rather than petrified) by the prospect of reconfirming my new frames. It felt less risky. Recall that I had perceived François as encouraging poor performance. This made me quite upset with the situation and with François too. But I had been avoiding talking to François about it and instead just venting at home. So I decided to confront François and scheduled a quick phone call on a Friday afternoon.

Unlike the first experiment, I did not assemble a table of response scenarios and tactics. Instead my plan was simply to be honest and open about how the situation was affecting me. The following two column case captures the essence of our conversation.

What I thought and felt	What was said
	Conversation starts off with small talk to break the ice.
	Jack: This is not easy for me to say because I enjoy working with you, I value your contributions, and I do not wish to alienate that relationship. Last weekend you sent an e-mail that made me angry. Not at you, but at the situation. You wrote: "Great changes, Felix!" That was a nice thing to say, but why did you say it? I perceived his contributions as too little, too late.

Wow, that was not exactly elegant but I do feel better having gotten that off my chest.	François: Okay, I know where you are going with this. Essentially we are encouraging this behavior by not calling it out.
Wow again!	Jack: Exactly, I feel we are encouraging this poor behavior. And I say *we* because I do it too. So essentially we are allowing the poor behavior by not holding each other accountable.
Am I being too assertive?	François: Let me tell you where I am coming from here. At the end of the week, I can either thank people for their efforts or I can call them out and plant a seed for bitterness. But I recognize the problem.
That is a good point! I bet you have the same frames of self-protection. I am feeling quite relieved to be free of my emotional burden, and comforted that my openness and honesty has not backfired as I feared it would.	Jack: Great. Would you be willing to share your thoughts on this situation and how we might handle it? I am interested in how you might approach this as a teammate, but also as a leader.
No high pulse rates, no sweats, nada.	Followed by a great conversation on team process; we don't jump to solutions but instead recognize the challenges and recognize that discussing the issue is the first step to resolving the issue.

Oh what's that? Encore, did you say? That experiment went rather swimmingly. Not only did I proactively confront François about a behavioral issue that was bothering me, but I also stayed true to my commitment to being open and honest without worrying too much about the plethora of possible responses. From the conversation, I inferred that François was applying his own defensive maneuvers to avoid planting "a seed for bitterness" that might grow into another killer Venus Flytrap of Team Destruction. To be fair, François was not exactly thankful that I confronted him. But the conversation made me feel better about the situation; it addressed an issue I felt was important, and it helped to reinforce my frames that being open and honest builds stronger (team) relationships.

Wrapping Up

Through this project I learned that I avoid confronting people in certain contexts. That avoidance has a profoundly negative effect on my emotions and relationships, and it stems from problematic frames that I developed early in life. By applying new frames to problematic interactions I was able to confront people about their behaviors and disconfirm my long-held assumption that confrontation damages relationships. Going forward, I anticipate experimenting more with my desired frames about confrontation until they become my de facto frames. As Cylon Number Six in Battlestar Galactica said: "Life has a melody, Gaius, a rhythm of notes which become your existence." My subconscious frames are my notes, and if I really try, I can write my own harmony.

Jack's inquiry is clearly just a beginning, but it captures some important aspects of how you can work on your craft. It shows the combination of deep analysis of self and seemingly small experiments with different actions. This combination occurs again and again in the most successful of my students' work. The deep self-analysis explains both how you are contributing to problematic interactions and why your own identity issues lead you to act the way you do. Identity issues run deep and are seldom overcome by analysis alone. That's why the small experiments are so helpful. They are small enough to not be so risky that you can't actually enact them and still big enough to provide some disconfirming data that helps you question your identity issues.

There's a lot of "how-to" management advice that offers ways of acting differently—usually with somewhat grandiose claims as to the results. And many of those methods can be very useful recipes for action. But without doing the self-analysis of why you don't act that way now – without understanding how your own past and identity issues lead you to behave in particular ways you are unlikely to be able to really enact those new behaviors. After all, you are a genius and you will figure out a way to enact the new behavior that comes from and conforms to your existing problematic frames. Even when you know your identity issues, there's a good chance that you will still manage to enact them when you come up with plans to act differently—it is part of being a genius. But since you are a genius you can figure that out as well and really act differently, especially if it's not too different.

So, the closing lesson here is the focus on the detail and the particular. The best way to become a great leader is to work on one interaction at a time, to take care of the details, and let the big picture emerge. That's not to say that you don't have to have the big picture in mind, but the order is important—the grand arc of your leadership tends to emerge from the many small leadership moments, not the other way around. There are of course, situations where it is harder—usually those that evoke a big emotional response and/or involve working against a big power differential. And those situations may be remembered as the important leadership moments in your life. But you and I know that those moments are only possible because you have honed your craft in all those other, not so memorable moments.

CHAPTER 10

The How, What, and Why of Leadership

This book has taken a particular approach to leadership—leadership as a craft that is realized in the interactions between people. The premise of the book is that all of us practice that craft, but few of us are masters. Few of us are masters because we don't work on getting better at that craft in the way that the masters of any craft consciously work on getting better at their craft. To get better requires conscious effort to get better, and it also requires the meta-skill of reflective practice—the ability to pay attention to your own practice and be aware of how your own actions contribute in both positive and negative ways to the results you want. I have focused on how to do that.

In focusing on how to get better at the craft of leadership, I have also largely avoided the questions of what leadership is and why you might want to lead. It says something about leadership that I can get to this point in a book about leadership without addressing the what or why questions. It says that leadership is one of those taken for granted things that we have difficulty defining in a way that we can all agree on, but we know it when we see it. Of course, that hasn't stopped countless academics and practitioners from trying to define it.[1] And there is something useful in attempts to define and conceptualize leadership. After all, as we have seen throughout this book, how we think about something—the frames (conscious and unconscious) we have—shape how we attend to things in the world, how we make sense of ambiguous data, and how we act in the world. So, of course, thinking about leadership differently can

---

[1] I have defined leadership a variety of times myself, for example, "We understand 'leadership' to be a collective phenomenon involving the mobilization of followers towards a goal or achievement of a purpose" (Taylor and Ladkin 2014, 96).

lead to us acting differently. Certainly, it is easy to see that someone trying to enact a charismatic form of leadership could behave very differently from someone who is trying to enact a form of servant leadership.

There is also the why of leadership. Why would you choose to enact a form of charismatic leadership versus choosing to enact a form of servant leadership? Why would you want to lead in the first place? In this book, I have included a form of the why question, namely, why are you the leader you are (in Chapter 8)? In exploring your life story you can identify the origins of both your own leadership challenges and your leadership strengths. Often buried within that exploration is the answer to the question of why you would want to lead or not lead in the first place. The bigger why question is fundamentally a philosophic issue about our values and what we want to do in our life. It is a question that is the foundation of ethical leadership action. It hinges upon our own understanding of the purpose of life and our place in the big picture. It is a question that cannot ever be definitively answered in a general way, but should always be asked. So, with that in mind, I end this book with a brief focus on the what question—what is it leaders do, how might we think of leadership and how might the skills of reflective practice discussed in this book do that.

What is Leadership?

Working from the idea that leadership is a creative process, I described five characteristics of leadership in my book *Leadership Craft, Leadership Art* namely: (1) it's a process, (2) there is a creative mindset, (3) it works best where there is passion, (4) it is collaborative, and (5) it exists within a domain. I spend the first half of the book exploring what that implies for leadership, so rather than repeat that here (I wouldn't want to spoil the book for you), I will simply say that it leads me to the conclusion that we should treat leadership as a craft, which was the starting point for this book.

My favorite conception of what leadership is comes from Keith Grint,[2] who writes about the four arts of leadership: (1) the philosophical art of identity, (2) the fine art of strategic vision, (3) the martial

---

[2] In *The Arts of Leadership* (Grint 2001).

art of organizational tactics, and (4) the performing art of persuasive communication. Grint identifies four distinct things that leaders do, while I identify five characteristics that leadership has. Both are ways to get at the what question of leadership. Not surprisingly, the basic framing of how to think about what leadership is, differs in the many different conceptions of leadership, putting the focus on whatever aspects of leadership the theorist is most interested in. As we try to define what leadership is, it becomes more and more apparent that the task is similar to the task faced by the six blind men who are trying to describe an elephant they encounter. One feels the elephant's trunk and describes it as a rope, another feels the elephant's side and describes it as a wall, and so on. Inherent in this story is the framing that if only they could see, the blind men would know what they were really dealing with.

But leadership isn't a thing that we can see, and even if we could, is an elephant really best defined by what you see? Within a given context, what the elephants eat, or that they mourn their dead may be far more important than the physical body we see. In this sense, there is no way to answer the question of what leadership is without first asking the question, why do you want to know? What is the context in which you ask the question? Meanwhile as we ask the question, for most of us our encounters with leadership more closely resemble the story of the six blind elephants who encounter a man. The first elephant says, "It feels kind of flat." The second elephant says, "It feels kind of flat." And so on as all six take their turn stepping on the man. Leadership can often leave us trampled in the grass and I suspect we all know what it looks like from that perspective.

I chose to describe leadership in terms of five characteristics because that allowed me to look at different aspects of leadership that I thought were important and generally not highlighted in most theories of leadership. I like Grint's four arts because it provides a framework for thinking about the various things that leaders do. At first blush only one of the four, the performing art of persuasive communication is clearly enacted in the interactions between people—which I claim is the medium of leadership. The fine art of making strategy and the martial art of tactics both seem like something that the leader can do by themselves—it is the *vision* work, setting the direction for the group, determining our goals, priorities, and what we shall do in both the near and long term. I would suggest that yes, an individual can create a strategy and individuals will certainly execute tactics, but neither is leadership until the strategy, tactics, or both are embraced by the group. It is the leader's job to make his or her strategy our strategy and this happens in the interactions between people. The same argument applies to tactics and identity.

Although I am arguing that it's not leadership until you've gotten others involved, Grint's four arts make it clear that there are things you do as a leader that are done individually even though they play out in the interactions between people. Leaders do make decisions. They may choose to make those decisions in consultation with others, but even if they choose to do that, at some point they have made a decision on their own to do so. The analysis of our own frames that is part of reflective practice is enormously helpful in making these decisions, especially when they are difficult and many possible sets of criteria exist for making the decision. In an extreme situation, it is useful to know that you have chosen to be guided by "the needs of the many outweigh the needs of the few" rather than "leave no one behind" or vice versa and why your values lead you to make that choice.

Leadership as Frame Creation

If I look at what these arts of leadership have in common, it is that all three (strategy, tactics, and identity) are about how we frame things. From this perspective, the what of leadership is all about creating common frames[3] that will drive our actions. It is both that simple and as we know from all of the work with our own frames, that difficult. Over the course of our lifetime we have developed frames that shape who we are (identity), what our long-term goals and values are (strategy), and how we will act in the moment (tactics). Many of these frames are unconscious and taken as fundamental truths. So to say that leadership is about creating and getting the group to act from common frames is to say that leadership is an extremely hard, if not outright impossible task. Of course, we don't have to have complete agreement because clearly that would be impossible.

---

[3] This argument comes primarily from the idea of leadership as sense making and sense giving (Gioia and Chittipeddi 1991).

To put such an emphasis on frames is to take a very psychological approach and suggest that frames drive actions. Philosophically, this approach is based in the Cartesian idea, "I think therefore I am." However, all of my work in reflective practice and theater has taught me that in reality I am not just my mind with my body following and enacting what I think, I am also my body and often my mind follows my body.[4] This is sometimes referred to as "fake it until you make it," but in the language I have been using, it is the simple recognition that we can choose to act differently and let new frames follow from that just as we can choose to frame things differently and let new actions follow from that. In reality, it is often best to take both approaches at the same time.

The implication for leadership is that reflective practice is not just what you do as a leader in order to get better at your craft. As a leader you should be leading reflective practice at an organizational level, you should be explicitly working with the organization to reflect on what frames are driving your actions and are they *good* frames? Are the organization's actions really in line with your frames or are they based in older, pre-existing *ghost* frames that haunt our subconscious?

It's not easy work. And just like the individual reflective practice illustrated in this book, it works best in practice when you are dealing with the specific situations and connecting those specifics to your broader values and beliefs. It takes time and effort when both are in short supply. There is always pressure to avoid doing the hard work of really digging into the questions of how our own actions contribute to problematic situations, how our own frames lead us to act that way and whether our frames really align with our values—are we being the person we want to be? These questions are all the more difficult at the organizational level—are we being the organization we want to be? Is it even possible to be the organization we want to be? Is there value for the world and can we harvest enough of that value to survive and thrive? How do we do that? How do we get others to share our dream? Those are the questions of identity, strategy, tactics, and communication—the questions that make leadership so difficult and so much fun.

---

[4] Amy Cuddy's (Carney, Cuddy, and Yap 2010) work on power poses makes this case empirically.

References

Adams, S. 1997. *The Dilbert Principle: A Cubicle's-Eye View of Bosses, Meetings, Management Fads & Other Workplace Afflictions*. New York: Harper Business.

Argyris, C. 1990. *Overcoming Organizational Defenses: Facilitating Organizational Learning*. Wellesley, MA: Allyn and Bacon.

Argyris, C. 1993. *Knowledge for Action: A Guide to Overcoming Barriers to Organizational Change*. San Francisco, CA: Jossey-Bass.

Argyris, C. 1999. *Flawed Advice and the Management Trap: How Managers Can Know When They're Getting Good Advice and When They're Not*. New York: Oxford University Press.

Argyris, C., R. Putnam, and D. Smith. 1985. *Action Science: Concepts, Methods, and Skills for Research and Intervention*. San Francisco, CA: Jossey-Bass.

Argyris, C., and D. Schön. 1974. *Theory in Practice: Increasing Professional Effectiveness*. 1st ed. San Francisco, CA: Jossey-Bass Publishers.

Argyris, C, and D. Schön. 1996. *Organizational Learning II: Theory, Method, and Practice*. Cambridge, MA: Addison-Wesley Publishing Company.

Austin, J.L. 1962. *How to Do Things with Words*. Oxford, United Kingdom: Clarendon Press.

Barile, M. 2012. *Curry Triangle*. Wolfram MathWorld. http://mathworld.wolfram.com/CurryTriangle.html (accessed on October 18, 2012).

Berthoin Antal, A. 2013. "Art Based Research for Engaging Not-Knowing in Organizations." In *Art As Research: Opportunities and Challenges*, ed. Shaun Mcniff. UK: Intellect Books/Chicago, IL: University of Chicago Press.

Carney, D.R, A.J.C. Cuddy, and A.J. Yap. 2010. "Power Posing Brief Nonverbal Displays Affect Neuroendocrine Levels and Risk Tolerance." *Psychological Science* 21, no. 10, pp. 1363–8.

Edwards, B. 1979. *The New Drawing on the Right Side of the Brain: A Course in Enhancing Creativity and Artistic Confidence*. New York: Tarcher.

Fershleiser, R., and L. Smith, eds. 2008. *Not Quite What I Was Planning: Six-Word Memoirs by Writers Famous and Obscure*. New York: Harper.

Fisher, D., and W.R. Torbert. 1995. *Personal and Organizational Transformations: The True Challenge of Continual Quality Improvement*. New York: McGraw-Hill.

Foster, P. 2013. "Collaborative Developmental Action Inquiry." In *Sage Encyclopedia of Action Research*, ed. Davod Coughlin. London, United Kingdom: Sage.

Gergen, K.J., and M. Gergen. 2004. *Social Construction: Entering the Dialogue.* Chagrin Falls, OH: Taos Institute Publications.

Gioia, D.A., and K. Chittipeddi. 1991. "Sensemaking and Sensegiving in Strategic Change Initiation." *Strategic Management Journal* 12, no. 6, pp. 433–48.

Grint, K. 2001. *The arts of leadership.* Oxford, United Kindgom: Oxford University Press.

Halpern, B.L., and K. Lubar. 2003. *Leadership Presence: Dramatic Techniques to Reach Out, Motivate, and Inspire.* New York: Gotham Books.

Hayakawa, S.I. 1941. *Language in Action.* New York: Harcourt, Brace, and Co.

Heller, J. 1961. *Catch-22.* New York: Simon & Schuster.

Keats, J. 1970. *Letters of John Keats (Oxford Letters & Memoirs).* New York: Oxford University Press.

Kegan, R. 1994. *In Over Our Heads: The Mental Demands Of Modern Life.* Cambridge, MA: Harvard University Press.

Kegan, R., and L. Lahey. 2001. *How the Way We Talk Can Change the Way We Work.* San Francisco, CA: Jossey-Bass.

Kegan, R., and L. Lahey. 2009. *Immunity to Change: How to Overcome it and Unlock the Potential in Yourself and Your Organization.* Boston, MA: Harvard Business Press.

Kelly, M. 2004. *The Rhythm of Life: Living Every Day with Passion and Purpose.* New York: Fireside.

Kelly, E.J. 2013. "Transformation in leadership, Part 1: A developmental study of Warren Buffett." *Integral Leadership Review* 13, no. 2, pp. 1–24.

Ladkin, D., and S.S. Taylor. 2010. "Enacting the 'True Self': Towards a Theory of Embodied Authentic Leadership." *Leadership Quarterly* 21, pp. 64–74.

Orwell, G. 1949. 1984. London, United Kingdom: Harcourt Brace.

Osgood, C.E, G.J. Suci, and P. Tannenbaum. 1957. *The Measurement of Meaning.* Chicago, IL: University of Illinois Press.

Perl, S. 2004. *Felt Sense: Writing with the body.* Portsmouth, NH: Boynton/Cook Heinemann.

Pugatch, J. 2006. *Acting Is a Job: Real-life Lessons About the Acting Business.* New York: Allworth Press.

Quinn, R.E. 2000. *Change the World: How Extraordinary People Can Accomplish Extraordinary Results.* San Francisco, CA: Jossey-Bass.

Rogers, C.R., and R.E. Farson. 1955. *Active Listening.* Chicago, IL: The University of Chicago.

Rooke, D., and W.R. Torbert. 2005. "Seven Transformations of Leadership." *Harvard Business Review* 83, no. 4, pp. 66–76.

Rudolph, J.W., S.S. Taylor, and E.G. Foldy. 2001. "Collaborative Off-Line Reflection: A Way to Develop Skill in Action Science and Action Inquiry." In *Handbook of Action Research: Participative Inquiry and Practice*, eds. Peter Reason and Hilary Bradbury, 405–412. London: Sage.

Rudolph, J.W., S.S. Taylor, and E.G. Foldy. 2006. "Collaborative Off-Line Reflection: A Way to Develop Skill in Action Science and Action Inquiry." In *Handbook of action research: Concise paperback edition*, eds. Peter Reason and Hilary Bradbury. London: Sage.

Schön, D.A. 1983. *The Reflective Practitioner: How Professionals Think in Action*. New York: Basic Books.

Schön, D.A. 1987. *Educating the Reflective Practicioner*. San Francisco, CA: Jossey-Bass.

Searle, J.R. 1969. *Speech Acts*. Cambridge, United Kingdom: Cambridge University Press.

Senge, P.M., C. Roberts, R.B. Ross, B.J. Smith, and Art Kleiner. 1994. *The Fifth Discipline Fieldbook: Strategies and Tools for Building a Learning Organization*. New York: Doubleday.

Sennett, R. 2008. *The Craftsman*. New Haven, CT: Yale University Press.

Smith, D.M. 1995. "Keeping a Strategic Dialogue Moving." Action Design. http://www.actiondesign.com/resources/readings/keeping-a-strategic-dialogue-moving4/

Smith, D.M. 2008. *Divide or Conquer: How Great Teams Turn Conflict Into Strength*. New York: Portfolio.

Smith, D.M. 2011. *The Elephant in the Room: How Relationships Make Or Break the Success of Leaders and Organizations*. San Francisco, CA: Jossey-Bass.

Springborg, C. 2010. "Leadership As Art: Leaders Coming to Their Senses." *Leadership* 6, no. 3, pp. 243–58.

Springborg, C. 2012. "Perceptual Refinement: Art-Based Methods in Managerial Education." *Organizational Aesthetics* 1, no. 1, pp. 116–37.

Stanislavski, C. 1936. *An Actor Prepares*. Translated by Elizabeth Reynolds Hapgood. New York: Routledge.

Stone, D., B. Patton, and S. Heen. 2000. *Difficult Conversations: How to Discuss What Matters Most*. New York: Penguin Books.

Taylor, S.S. 2005. "My Mother, My Sweater: An Aesthetics of Action Perspective for Teaching Communication." *Journal of Organizational Behavior Education* 1, no. 1, pp. 57–72.

Taylor, S.S. 2012. *Leadership Craft, Leadership Art*. New York: Palgrave Macmillan.

Taylor, S.S. 2013a. "Authentic Leadership and the Status Trap." In *Authentic Leadership: Concepts, Coalescences and Clashes*, eds. Donna Ladkin and Chellie Spiller, 176–87. London: Edward Elgar.

Taylor, S.S. 2013b. "What is Organizational Aesthetics?" *Organizational Aesthetics* 2, no. 1, pp. 30–32.

Taylor, S.S. 2015. "Open Your Heart." In *The Physicality of Leadership: Gesture, Entanglement, Taboo, Possibilities*, eds. Donna Ladkin and Steven S. Taylor. London: Emerald.

Taylor, S.S., and I. Carboni. 2008. "Technique & Practices from the Arts: Expressive Verbs, Feelings, and Action." In *The SAGE Handbook of New*

Approaches in Management and Organization, eds. David Barry and Hans Hansen, 220–28. London, United Kingdom: Sage.

Taylor, S.S., and D. Ladkin. 2014. "Leading as Craft-Work: The Role of Studio Practices in Developing Artful Leaders." *Scandinavian Journal of Management* 30, no. 1, pp. 95–103.

Torbert, W.R. 1972. *Learning from Experience: Toward Consciousness.* New York: Columbia University Press.

Torbert, W.R. 1987. *Managing the Corporate Dream: Restructuring for Long-Term Success.* Homewood, IL: Dow Jones-Irwin.

Torbert, W.R. 1991. *The Power of Balance: Transforming Self, Society, and Scientific Inquiry.* Newbury Park, CA: Sage.

Torbert, W.R., and Associates. 2004. *Action Inquiry: The Secret of Timely and Transforming Leadership.* San Francisco, CA: Berrett-Koehler.

Torbert, W.R., and M. Stacey. 2009. "Action Inquiry: Transforming Leadership in the Midst of Action." Paper presented at the Authentic Leadership in Action Shambhala Summer Institute, Nova Scotia.

Torbert, W.R., and S.S. Taylor. 2008. "Action Inquiry: Interweaving Multiple Qualities of Attention for Timely Action." In *Handbook of Action Research*, eds. Peter Reason and Hilary Bradbury, 239–51. 2nd ed. London, United Kindgom: Sage.

Whitehead, J. 1989. "Creating a Living Educational Theory from Questions of the Kind, 'How Do I Improve My Practice?'" *Cambridge Journal of Education* 19, no. 1, pp. 41–52.

Index

OTHER TITLES IN THE HUMAN RESOURCE MANAGEMENT AND ORGANIZATIONAL BEHAVIOR COLLECTION

- *Developing Employee Talent to Perform: People Power* by Kim Warren
- *Culturally Intelligent Leadership: Leading Through Intercultural Interactions* by Mai Moua
- *Letting People Go: The People-Centered Approach to Firing and Laying Off Employees* by Matt Shlosberg
- *The Five Golden Rules of Negotiation* by Philippe Korda
- *Cross-Cultural Management* by Veronica Velo
- *Conversations About Job Performance: A Communication Perspective on the Appraisal Process* by Michael E. Gordon and Vernon Miller
- *How to Coach Individuals, Teams, and Organizations to Master Transformational Change: Surfing Tsunamis* by Stephen K. Hacker
- *Managing Employee Turnover: Dispelling Myths and Fostering Evidence-Based Retention Strategies* by David Allen and Phil Bryant
- *Mastering Self-Motivation: Bringing Together the Academic and Popular Literature* by Michael Provitera
- *Effective Interviewing and Information Gathering: Proven Tactics to Improve Your Questioning Skills* by Thomas Diamante
- *Managing Expatriates: A Return on Investment Approach* by Yvonne McNulty
- *Fostering Creativity in Self and the Organization: Your Professional Edge* by Eric W. Stein
- *Designing Creative High Power Teams and Organizations: Beyond Leadership* by Eric W. Stein
- *Creating a Pathway to Your Dream Career: Designing and Controlling a Career Around Your Life Goals* by Tom Kucharvy
- *Leader Evolution: From Technical Expertise to Strategic Leadership* by Alan Patterson
- *Followership: What It Takes to Lead* by James H. Schindler
- *The Search For Best Practices: Doing the Right Thing the Right Way* by Rob Reider
- *Competencies at Work: Providing a Common Language for Talent Management* by Bruce Griffiths and Enrique Washington
- *Manage Your Career: 10 Keys to Survival and Success When Interviewing and on the Job, Second Edition* by Vijay Sathe

Announcing the Business Expert Press Digital Library

Concise e-books business students need for classroom and research

This book can also be purchased in an e-book collection by your library as

- a one-time purchase,
- that is owned forever,
- allows for simultaneous readers,
- has no restrictions on printing, and
- can be downloaded as PDFs from within the library community.

Our digital library collections are a great solution to beat the rising cost of textbooks. E-books can be loaded into their course management systems or onto students' e-book readers.
The **Business Expert Press** digital libraries are very affordable, with no obligation to buy in future years. For more information, please visit **www.businessexpertpress.com/librarians**. To set up a trial in the United States, please email **sales@businessexpertpress.com**.

CPSIA information can be obtained
at www.ICGtesting.com
Printed in the USA
FSOW02n1710110917
38645FS